Songs of the Servant King

A Prophetical Anthology

A study in Isaiah's Servant Songs
Prophetical & Devotional

by **Samuel T. Carson**

Books by the same author
"***The Long Road Home***"
(a commentary on Ezra & Nehemiah)
"***The Genesis Brides***"
and other works.

BELFAST, NORTHERN IRELAND
GREENVILLE, USA

Songs of the Servant King

ISBN 1 84030 110 4

Ambassador Publications
a division of
Ambassador Productions Ltd.
Providence House
Ardenlee Street,
Belfast,
BT6 8QJ
Northern Ireland
www.ambassador-productions.com

Emerald House
427 Wade Hampton Blvd.
Greenville
SC 29609, USA
www.emeraldhouse.com

Contents

Meet the Servant King

While any *rags to riches* story is enough to excite our idle curosity and to arouse our interest, we become confused when we attempt to comprehend the self-humbling of the Son of God. That the Sovereign of the universe should become a man, assume the form and role of a servant and tread this earth in human weakness, is quite beyond the range of our natural understanding. Even to this day, two thousand years after the event, angels and devout men are constrained to bow in reverent worship at the implications of this mystery.

Adam was the first man. He had been formed to execute God's government in the earth. But he failed and because of his disobedience he was set aside. And then in the fullness of time a second man appeared, a last Adam, of whom it was said, "He shall not fail." Unlike other men He did not begin to be when He was born, for His going forth was from of old, even from everlasting. The second man was the Lord from heaven.

There are four passages in the second part of Isaiah's prophecy which when taken together form a prophetical anthology. These passages are commonly referred to as Isaiah's Servant Songs. And the four Songs introduce us to this remarkable man and give us an overview of His task.

Presented to us in language that has been described as some of the most beautiful poetry in Hebrew literature, the Songs themselves pass before the mind as a series of prophetic visions. They are skilfully woven into the second part of Isaiah; and while they are not the total story, they are the pivotal points on which the story turns. For this reason it is not inappropriate to lift them out of their immediate settings and to bring them together.

Like many of the Psalms, the Songs are so clearly messianic it is not difficult to see their reference to the Lord Jesus Christ, and their ultimate fulfilment in Him. Intertwined and developed in each of the four songs there are two distinct ideas. The first is the servanthood of Christ; and the second is His sovereignty. Hence the title of this volume, *Songs of the Servant King.*

The Servant Songs - An Overview

The First Song (Isa. 42:1-9)

The first song proclaims the Servant's purpose in coming into the world. He came to accomplish salvation and to establish justice and righteousness in the earth. The song unfolds both His manner and His methods, and reveals them to be utterly different from those commonly espoused by men of the world. Any doubt about the Servant's identity is dispelled by Matthew's use of this first song for he quotes it at length as an actual description of the Lord Jesus Christ. (See Matt.12:17-21.)

The Second Song (Isa. 49:1-12)

The second song calls attention to the seeming failure of the Servant in His initial overtures to the nation of Israel. But then it goes on to inform us that, although initially rejected by Israel, the Servant's mission will be renewed and, in the end, it will be extended to bring the salvation of God to the nations. It would appear that the aged

Simeon had this second song in his mind at the time of Christ's birth. For when the infant Jesus was presented to him in the temple, he spoke of Him as "a light to lighten the Gentiles, and the glory of thy people, Israel" (Luke 2:32).

The Third Song (Isa. 50:1-11)

In very graphic language, the third song highlights the afflictions and tribulations that would be involved in the Servant's mission to the messianic nation. He would suffer multiplied indignities at the hands of the very people whose lasting good He had come to seek. The Lord Jesus was surely thinking of all the venom envisaged in this third servant song when He declared, "It is written of the Son of man, that he must suffer many things, and be set at nought" (Mark 9:12).

The Fourth Song (Isa. 52:13 - 53:12)

One of the predictions of the fourth song was that when Messiah came, He would be 'reckoned among the transgressors' and Jesus specifically applied this reference to Himself (Luke 22:37). But the fourth and final song also celebrates His vindication. After all the sufferings He endured, both during His life and in His death, His days are prolonged, He sees His seed and the pleasure of the Lord prospers in His hand.

In the marvellous providence of God, the Ethiopian eunuch was reading this fourth song as he journeyed through the desert, homeward bound from Jerusalem. The same providence guided Philip, the evangelist, to make contact with him, and beginning at that same scripture he preached unto him, *Jesus* (Acts 8:35). Clearly, Philip had no difficulty in seeing *Jesus* in the fourth servant song.

The servant songs, therefore, are a series of telling revelations concerning Him of whom Moses and the prophets wrote. They centre on an individual whose personality is so described that the plain reader, especially one familiar with the New Testament, can have little hesitation in identifying as the Lord Jesus Christ, Israel's promised Messiah, and our wonderful Saviour.

But the songs also serve to emphasise that the purposes of God are revealed in the context of two advents, and not just one. It is a self-evident fact, and one we are all too acutely aware of, that the promises made at the time of the first advent, 'peace on earth and goodwill among men,' have not yet been achieved. The reality is that everything is on hold, awaiting the second advent. We will signally fail to understand the first advent, if we do not see that it was intended to prepare for a second. It is with great subtlety that both the advents are woven into each of the servant songs.

Taken together, these four songs declare that everything implied in the divine counsels will yet be brought to pass. All will be fulfilled in association with the Lord Jesus Christ, when He comes again in power and great glory, and when He is revealed as the King of all kings and the Lord of all lords.

1 Behold my servant, whom I uphold; my elect, in whom my soul delights; I have put my Spirit upon him; He shall bring forth [justice] to the [nations].
2 He shall not cry, nor lift up, nor cause his voice to be heard in the street.
3 A bruised reed shall he not break, and the smoking flax shall he not quench; he shall bring forth [justice] in truth.
4 He shall not fail nor be discouraged, till he have set [justice] in the earth; and the isles shall wait for his law.
5 Thus saith God, the Lord, he who created the heavens, and stretched them out; he who spread forth the earth, and that which comes out of it; he who gives breath unto the people upon it, and spirit to them that walk in it:
6 I, the Lord, have called you in righteousness, and will hold your hand, and will keep you, and will give you for a covenant of the people, for a light to the [nations].
7 To open the blind eyes, to bring out the prisoners from the prison, and those who sit in darkness out of the prison house.
8 I am the Lord: that is my name; and my glory will I not give to another, neither my praise to [carved] images.
9 Behold, the former things are come to pass, and new things do I declare; before they spring forth I tell you of them.

1st Servant Song: Isaiah 42:1-9

The *First Song*

This song follows the introductory statement with which the second part of Isaiah's prophecy begins. It reveals the Servant King in the perfection of His person. And, from a messianic standpoint, it informs us of His mission in coming into the world. He will establish a kingdom of universal peace and justice among the nations.

The Messianic King

Behold my Servant (v.1)

Sixty-six books make up the sacred canon of scripture. These divide into two parts, thirty-nine in the Old Testament, and twenty-seven in the New. In the same way the prophecy of Isaiah may be divided into two component parts. There are thirty-nine chapters in the first part, and these are followed by a further twenty-seven. The sixty-six chapters complete the prophecy of Isaiah, just as the sixty-six books complete the canon of scripture. For this reason the book of Isaiah is often referred to as the Bible in minature.

Sometimes called the evangelical prophet, Isaiah has been the subject of considerable controversy. For the most part this has raged around the question of authorship. The term '*Deutero-Isaiah*' (meaning the second Isaiah) encapsulates the issue. While accepting the Isaiahic authorship of the first part of the prophecy, the critics argue that the second part was the work of another writer, or perhaps even of several others.

Behind the debate one can sense an inability, or perhaps it is an unwillingness, to accept that anyone could speak with such clarity, so many years beforehand, of the events referred to in the second part of this prophecy. It is argued, for instance, that the many things said about Cyrus, the king of Persia, could not have been known to Isaiah, who had died about one hundred years before Cyrus was born.

But what some see as a weakness, we look upon as an evidence of divine revelation. We believe that "Known unto God are all His works from the beginning of the world" (Acts 15:18). That Isaiah's predictions concerning Cyrus, were fulfilled in such detail is simply another instance of the total veracity of the prophetic word. In any event, it is from this position we are taking up *the Servant Songs.* Our intention is to learn from them about Him of whom Isaiah wrote, as we believe, in both parts of his prophecy.

Other Servants

It is not our purpose to discuss the different ways in which the Servant Songs themselves have been understood. Some identify the Servant with the prophet himself, and some link Him with Cyrus. (See Isa.44:28.) As we have noted, Cyrus was at that time, the still future king of Persia. In due course, he became known as Cyrus the Great when he overcame the Babylonian empire and established his own in its place.

Others view the Servant in a corporate way, representing a group of people, possibly a remnant within Israel, or even the nation itself considered ideally. But ideal Israel has never existed, and no remnant within Israel has ever come close to achieving what is claimed for the Servant of these songs.

A cursory glance at a concordance will show that the term 'servant' rarely occurs in the first part of Isaiah, and when it does, the servant in view is clearly identified. It is also worth noting that when the prophet has other servants in view, he usually identifies them by name, e.g. *my servant Eliakim, my servant David, etc..* But in the second part of Isaiah, the word occurs about twenty times.

Laying aside the references which are the subject of this book, the term is usually applied to the nation of Israel. (See Isa. 41:8-10; 43:22 etc.) That this is so, seems to be confirmed by the prophet's repeated and quite specific mention of that nation by name. (See Isa. 44:1,2,21; 48:20.) There is also a somewhat obscure reference to a blind servant. (See Isa. 42:19.) On this interpretations vary, but the weight of opinion is that this too is a covert reference to the nation of Israel.

Israel as God's servant

In a later chapter, we shall consider the reasons behind God's choice of Israel to be His servant. But in the meantime, we will simply point out that Israel had been intended to serve God in two principle ways. In the first place, the nation was to be a witness against the evils of idolatry. And secondly, Israel was to be a testimony to the surrounding nations, showing them the blessedness of a people whose God is Jehovah. On both counts the chosen people proved a lamentable failure. (See Ezk.8:5-18.)

Here in these songs our attention is turned to an individual who, in order to serve God where Israel had so signally failed, voluntarily assumed the role and status of a servant. Besides affirming that the mission of this heaven-sent Servant will be accomplished, the prophet asserts the impossibility of any breakdown on His part. With emphasis Isaiah insists, "He shall not fail" (Isa.42:4).

Jesus Christ - The Perfect Servant

In reading these songs we are assuming, what we have already established, that the Servant they set forth is none other than Jesus Christ, our Lord. Clearly the Lord Jesus was God's Servant in a sense in which no one else before or since, has been or could be. We might add, that this has been the usually accepted view of evangelical expositors across the years. (See notes at the end of this chapter.)

The servant ideal found its supreme and comprehensive expression in the Lord Jesus Christ. And the first song asserts this uniqueness in a simple and uncomplicated designation, *Behold my Servant* (Isa.42:1). Besides being a title of honour, this description also carries royal overtones. It is reminiscent of the terms used to identify Saul and David to the prophet Samuel, when they were respectively anointed to become the first kings of Israel.

When the prophet first set eyes on Saul, the Lord said, "Behold, the man whom I spoke to you of! This same shall reign over my people" (1Sam.9:17). A similar exchange took place when David was anointed.(See 1Sam.16:12,13.) And a comparable expression was used of Zerubbabel, who led the exiles back from Babylon. "Behold, the man whose name is the Branch; and he shall grow up out of his place, and he shall build the temple of the Lord" (Zech.6:12). Zerubbabel, was descended from David and was a prince of Judah. He is mentioned in the Lord's geneology (Matt.1:13). And He should certainly be viewed as a type of Christ, the Messiah of Israel.

Following his quite abrupt introduction of the Lord Jesus as the obedient and perfect Servant of Jehovah, Isaiah goes on to emphasise His self-humbling, His manner of living, and His purpose in coming into the world. He did not come to judge but to save; nor did He come to be served, but to serve, and to give His life a ransom for many. (See Matt.20:28.) His purpose in coming is summed up in these two words, to serve and to give.

Girded with a Towel

In a curtain raiser to what is usually referred to as the upper room ministry, the Lord Jesus engaged in a very practical and most memorable act of service. What He did, besides instructing the disciples, graphically illustrated the reality of His self-humbling and His servanthood. Laying aside His garments, He girded himself with a towel. And then pouring water into a basin He proceeded to wash the disciples' feet. (See John 13:1-17.)

What an incredible spectacle, the Lord of Glory, lately become a man, stooping to perform the most menial of servile tasks! Could anything be more incongruous? The master taking the place of the slave, and doing all in the full consciousness of who He was, of where He had come from, and where He was going. The inspired record says, "Jesus, knowing that the Father had given all things into His hands, and that He was come from God, and went to God, laid aside His garments ... " (John13:3).

One could be excused for thinking that Paul was actually visualising that upper room scene when he wrote what is considered by many to be the greatest Christological passage in the sacred writings. "Who being in the form of God ... took upon Him the form of a servant ... and being found in fashion as a man, He humbled Himself, and became obedient unto death, even the death of the cross" (Phil.2:6-11). This scripture is regularly spoken of as the key statement on the servant character of our Saviour.

The Servant's Status

In attempting to comprehend this amazing phenomenon we must, of course, distinguish between the servanthood and slavery of Biblical times, and the slavery so successfully countered by people like William Wilberforce. In ancient times, the relationship between a Hebrew slave and his master was established within a legal framework, which bestowed rights and enjoined responsibilities on both parties.

For instance, a slave who had completed the tenure of his service still had the legal right to remain in his master's house if he did not wish to leave. And if he decided to leave, then his master had certain clearly defined and legally established rights as well. (See Ex.21:1-6.) But having said that, it still has to be recognised that even in those days, the Hebrew slave or servant found himself at the bottom of the social pile.

All this throws into bold relief the striking way in which the Lord of Glory, by taking a servant's place, sanctified the humblest of occupations among men. When the Son of God assumed a human form, the glory of the only begotten of the Father was displayed on earth in situations of complete and total lowliness. With complete sincerity the Lord Jesus was able to say, "I am meek and lowly in heart" (Matt.11:29).

A Servant still

But besides His renowned servant character at the time of His first coming, we must not overlook the very practical and precious truth that during this present interval between the advents, our Lord is also engaged in the service of His people. Even now, while in the heavenly sanctuary, the Lord Jesus serves His people as their intercessor and advocate. "Wherefore, He is able also to save them to the uttermost that come unto God by Him, seeing He ever lives to make intercession for them" (Hebs.7.25).

Moreover, we know that when He comes again, He will retain this servant character. Of that hour it is written, "Blessed are those servants, whom the Lord, when He comes, shall find watching; verily I say unto you, that He shall gird Himself, and make them to sit down to eat, and will come forth and serve them." (See Luke 12:37.) We could scarcely imagine such future service, had it not been so plainly affirmed in the scriptures. We are able therefore, to see three dimensions to the servanthood of Christ; the first belongs to the past, the second to the present, and the third to the future.

Kingdom Service

The subject, however, is even greater than that, for this perfect Servant will also be God's instrument in Israel's promised national recovery and restoration. At His coming again, He will establish the messianic kingdom; the reign of peace and of righteousness, so long foretold by the Hebrew prophets. And through restored Israel He will bring the blessing of Abraham to the Gentile nations. Without doubt, the servanthood of Christ will take on fuller and wider meanings as these things unfold.

In a certain sense the call to "*Behold my Servant*" sums up the entire revelation given to us in the scriptures. We might say that this is what the Bible is all about. In the previous chapter the living God had called to the nations, "Keep silence before me" (Isa.41:1). And now in this first song the reason for such silence is given in the poignant summons to "Behold my Servant."

By the pressures of modern living we are all exposed to a constant babble of voices. And the clamour, unprecedented in any previous generation, is intensifying all the time. It is necessary, indeed it is vital, for us to withdraw ourselves from the world's mad strife, and take time to *Behold Him*, our Servant-King. Chosen in the eternal counsels, in the fullness of time He appeared in human form and in a servant character. He came to do the Father's will. And in the end, the pleasure of the Lord shall prosper in His hand.

Footnotes:

Isa.42. "We place this passage by the side of those passages that refer to the individual Messiah. In Matt.3:17 and Matt.17:5 the reference to this passage is so obvious that the Evangelist must be viewed as indicating that this passage is a distinct prophecy concerning Messiah." (Leupold Vol.2. p.61.)
"It is an ideal picture of the future - the future Christ." (Delitzsch p.165.)

Isa.49. "Our approach to the problem of the identity of the Servant is that he is ... the Messiah." (Leupold Vol. 2. p.176.)
"He who speaks with such compelling authority is the Messiah as head of his people." (Young Vol.3. p.267.)

Isa. 50. "In chapter 49.vs 1-6 the beginning of the continuous section of which these verses are part, a transition is made from Israel as collectively the ideal servant of the Lord, to a personal Servant, whose office is to bring Jacob again to him. The text of v.4 gives us a striking view of the purpose of Messiah's mission and of his training and preparation for it." (Maclaren Vol.2. p15/16.)

Isa. 53. "The evidence in favour of the Messianic interpretation comes now to be considered; and that is indeed overwhelmingly powerful. The manner in which this oracle is quoted in the New Testament is of itself quite sufficient to settle the question." (John Brown 'Sufferings and Glory of Messiah' Part 2. p.154.)

The *First Song*

The Messianic King (contd.)

I have put My Spirit upon Him (v.1)

The Two Advents

For a proper understanding of the prophetic scriptures in general, and of the servant songs in particular, it is vital to keep in mind the two advents of Christ, and to distinguish between them. When the prophets of Israel anticipated Messiah's coming they saw things in terms of suffering and of glory. And it is not unfair to say that they could not always or easily come to terms with what, at times, appeared to them to be contradictory concepts. (See1Pet.1:10-12.)

From our perspective, of course, we are able to discern a marvellous and meaningful harmony in those prophetic visions. We know that, far from being contradictory, the sufferings and the glory, perfectly complement each other. Positioned between the advents, we can see quite plainly how the sufferings related to Messiah's first advent, and how the glory looks on to the second.

The Lord Jesus Himself was careful to draw a clear distinction between the two advents. His somewhat confused companions on the Emmaus Road, unable to do this, had already convinced themselves that their hopes and aspirations had been crushed by His dying. And so overcome were they with sorrow, they even failed to recognise the stranger who had joined them on their journey home.

Although He knew their sorrows, He would hear them from their own lips. And then in His own time He quickly corrected their thinking with a single, searching question: "Ought not Christ to have suffered these things, and to enter into His glory?" (Luke 24:26) It was a rhetorical question, and He answered it in the fullest possible manner. Even as they walked along that dreary road, the sufferings were already past, they belonged to the immediate past; but the glory belonged to another advent, and it still lay in the future.

Both the advents are constantly in view in the servant songs. For instance, in the first verse of this first song two quite separate statements lie immediately before us. (i) *"I have put my Spirit upon Him;"* and (ii) *"He shall bring forth justice to the nations."* (Isa.42:1) It is important to distinguish between these two statements. On the surface, they seem fairly lucid, but on closer examination we discover a time-gap between them; an extended period, that has now been drawn out to around two thousand years.

The Baptism

The first statement, "*I have put my Spirit upon Him*," points directly to our Lord at the time of His first advent, and specifically to His baptism in the river Jordan. John the Baptist said at the time, "I saw the Spirit descending from heaven like a dove, and it abode upon Him. And I knew Him not; but He that sent me to baptize with water, the same said to me, 'Upon whom you shall see the Spirit descending, and remaining on Him, the same is He who baptizes with the Holy Spirit'. And I saw, and bore witness that this is the Son of God" (John 1:32-34).

It is of more than passing interest, that here in the first song, as well as in the record of Jesus' baptism, there is more than a hint of the doctrine of the Trinity. "I [*the Father*] have put my Spirit [*the Spirit*] upon Him [*the Son*]" (v.1). The Scriptures consistently reveal a triune mode to the Divine existence. Three persons, Father, Son and Holy Spirit, co-existent, co-equal and co-eternal; yet one God, who is blessed for evermore. The human mind cannot comprehend or adequately explain the doctrine of the Trinity. It is a revelation before which faith bows in humble adoration.

The very nature of the Trinity means that God can inflict punishment, and at the same time, He can bear that same punishment. And this is precisely what happened when God was in Christ reconciling the world unto Himself. (See 2Cor.5:19.) Through the mystery of the incarnation and the miracle of the virgin birth, the eternal Son, the second person of this blessed and holy Trinity humbled Himself and became a man. In doing so, He took upon Himself the form and status of a Servant, and became obedient unto death, even the death of the cross. Here is a condescension so stupendous, we freely admit it to be beyond our finite powers.

Down from His glory,
Ever living story,
My God, and Saviour came,
And Jesus was His name.

The prophet's use of the past tense: "I *have* put my Spirit upon Him" is a feature of the prophetic scriptures. The reference was not to an event already fulfilled, for that was still some seven hundred years distant, but to an event certain of fulfilment. Its eventual fulfilment in Christ, centuries later, is further proof that God is true to His word. It also underscores the amazing precision of that word, and it is a telling aide memoire to us that the scripture cannot be broken.

Jesus and the Holy Spirit

In Isaiah's writings there are three deeply meaningful references to the influence of the Holy Spirit in our Saviour's earthly life. The first has to do with His incarnation, the second and central reference is to His baptism, while the third points to the beginning of His public ministry. The final reference has in view the object, the nature, and the execution of that ministry. (See Isa.11:1, 42:1 & 61:1.)

It was always true that our Saviour had the Spirit upon Him, and that in a plenary sense, for "God gave not the Spirit by measure unto Him" (John 3:34). In keeping with this we read that Jesus was "full of the Spirit," that He was "led by the Spirit," and that He moved in "the power of the Spirit." In addition, we are told that He preached as one anointed by the Spirit, for He said, "the Spirit of the Lord is upon me, because He has anointed me to preach the gospel to the poor" (Luke 4:1,14,18). Herein lay the secret behind the Father's engaging tribute, "*My servant ... in whom my soul delights*."

This was the Father's first public demonstration of delight in His Son. Coming at the time of His baptism the anointing was more than just a signal, showing approval of the act of baptism, it was a public expression of the Father's pleasure in the life of the Lord Jesus during the thirty years that had passed. The anointing was also an open recognition of Jesus as Jehovah's Servant. It signalled the inauguration of His public ministry. It was a most striking endorsement, and it marked His induction to the messianic service so clearly envisaged by all the prophets. (See Isa.61:1,2.)

It should be the settled aim of every believer to imitate this Servant, and to walk as He walked, for He is our pattern in all things and our final exemplar. Our enablement lies in the gift of the indwelling Holy Spirit, given to us at the point of conversion. The Spirit's primary ministry is always to work in us and through us causing our lives to be an expression of the life of Jesus to the glory of God. The essential prerequisite to this is stated in the apostolic exhortation, "Grieve not the Holy Spirit of God, by whom you are sealed unto the day of redemption" (Eph.4:30).

The *First Song*

The Messianic Kingdom

He shall bring forth justice (i)

The final statement at the end of verse one says, "*He shall bring forth justice to the nations.*" Elsewhere we are told that He came to put away sin, and to destroy the works of the Devil. But in this song, the Messianic purpose is before us and so the prophet proclaims the Servant's goal in terms of establishing a just and lasting rule among the nations.

The initial assertion is then expanded, "He shall bring forth justice in truth" (v.3), and further, "He shall not fail nor be discouraged, till He has set justice in the earth and the isles shall wait for His law" (v.4). This startling assertion about justice being established in the earth, encapsulates the main theme of the first song and is repeated three times for emphasis.

Peace with justice is a priceless ideal even if it has proved strangely elusive to the nations. It loomed large in Isaiah's vision from the beginning. He speaks of a time when the nations will "beat their swords into plowshares, and their spears into pruning hooks; and nation shall not lift up sword against nation, neither shall they learn war any more" (Isa.2:4).

The long and chequered history of human government suggests that such an order will not be achieved either by evolutionary processes or by schemes of man's devising. Peace conferences and arbitration agreements doubtless have their place in the short term, but their attainments are always limited and in the end they usually wither on the vine.

Only when He comes whose right it is to reign, will the open-handed and transparent justice be realised that is envisaged in this song. Not until then will the corrupt and baneful practices of government in the interest of the governing classes, rather than of the governed, be no more.

Messiah's rule will be with equity and benevolence, He shall judge righteously among all peoples. Since righteousness is the foundation of God's throne, it follows that nothing short of a righteous order in the earth can satisfy that throne.

Peace with Justice

It scarcely needs to be argued that this song predicates a concept of justice beyond anything our world knows today. Justice here is not a mere papering over of the cracks, nor is it a dictatorial subjugation of dissent, and it is more than just a handing down of punishment or retribution. It is a fundamental putting right of whatever may be wrong. Its root idea denotes a righteous order in every sense of that term.

This exalted concept of justice, embracing the entire Gentile world, is a prospect that projects our minds beyond the Church of this present age, and beyond God's immediate designs for Israel as a nation, to the establishment of Messiah's reign. Isaiah is quite clearly anticipating conditions that will only obtain in the earth during the period of our Lord's millennial kingdom. In what is conventionally known as the Lord's prayer, Jesus taught His disciples to pray for such a kingdom. He said, "After this manner, therefore, pray ye: … *Thy kingdom come*, Thy will be done in earth, as it is in heaven" (Matt.6:10).

Some prefer to render this central petition of the prayer in terms of the kingship or reign of God. They see the term *kingdom* as rather limiting for it is apt to suggest to our minds a certain area or territory, like the United Kingdom of Great Britian and Northern Ireland. But we shall see that while this sits easily with the kingdom of God in some of its aspects, there are other aspects of the kingdom that imply definite territorial dimensions. The theocratic kingdom of David and Solomon was one, and the coming messianic kingdom will be another.

Several things about that future kingdom will become evident as we proceed. We shall find that its earthly centre will be Jerusalem, the city of the great king. Its citizens will be the people of Israel and the Gentile nations, and it will govern the whole earth. We shall discover as well that the paramount place among the nations in those days will be accorded to Israel, restored to the Lord and to the land, and no longer divided into ten tribes and two, but one nation again.

Messiah's Reign

The period of that future dominion of Christ is usually called '*The Millennial Reign*' or '*The Messianic Kingdom*.' It is not difficult to establish that the coming reign of Christ will be for a millennium, a period of one thousand years. In fact, the one thousand year reign of Christ is referred to no fewer than six times in as many verses in a single chapter. (See Rev.20:1-7.) The details given are so explicit, it does not seem possible that the reference could be misunderstood. Even the very people who will reign with Christ are also plainly identified.

The saints of the first resurrection will reign with Him. Hence we read, "They lived and reigned with Christ a thousand years. But the rest of the dead lived not again until the thousand years were finished. This is the first resurrection. Blessed and holy is he that has part in the first resurrection; on such the second death has no power, but they shall be priests of God and of Christ, and shall reign with Him a thousand years." (See Rev. 20:4-6.)

We should be wary of attempts to make this scripture mean something it does not say. On the one hand, the first resurrection has to be a literal and physical resurrection since the persons raised had, in fact, died in a literal and physical sense. Moreover, the first part of the first resurrection has already taken place in the resurrection of Christ, and that was a literal and physical resurrection. (See

1Cor.15:23.) On the other hand, this resurrection cannot be called a general resurrection, for we are told that one thousand years will intervene between the first resurrection, and the raising of the rest of the dead.

Predicting the millennial period the prophet Isaiah declared, "The redeemer shall come to Zion, and unto those who turn from transgression in Jacob" (Isa.59:20). He went on to say, "Arise, shine; for your light is come, and the glory of the Lord is risen upon you. For, behold, the darkness shall cover the earth, and gross darkness the people, but the Lord shall arise upon you, and His glory shall be seen upon you. And the Gentiles shall come to your light, and kings to the brightness of your rising" (Isa.60:1-3).

Terms and Titles

That such a kingdom will be instituted at the second advent seems to have been the near universal belief of the early Church, and the concept of such a kingdom being established in the earth is very largely accepted by believing people today. For the most part, differences among them on this topic centre on points of detail, such as the manner and timing of its establishment, and how it should be designated.

On the latter point, it is always helpful to keep in mind that terms are often used in a variety of senses. This is true of scripture, as it is of any writings. Any given term or text, therefore, should be considered in the light of its immediate context first, for only then can it properly be related to the same term in other contexts. If we fail at this point, we will surely distort the scriptures to our own confusion.

Israel

A notable example of this is the use of the term *'Israel'*. The word was first used as a personal name for Jacob. Then it came to represent the nation that developed from his twelve sons, the twelve tribes of Israel. Later still, after the great schism following Solomon's death, it came to denote the ten northern tribes, and to distinguish them from the two southern tribes now known as Judah. It also appears in at least one reference, as a title given to Messiah. (See Isa.49:3.)

The World

There are a great many references in scripture to *'the world'* but this term too, when rightly understood, represents several quite different ideas. Sometimes it means the earth or the land, at other times it stands for the inhabitants of the planet. And it is even used to designate a given age, a distinct period within time, which is to be distinguished from other ages. *The kingdom* is yet another term of which this is also true.

Aspects of the Kingdom

The Lord Jesus told His hearers, "The kingdom of God is *within* you" (Luke 17.21). This is correctly rendered in the margin of the *n.i.v.* "The kingdom of God is *among* you." It was present in the person of the King who was among them, but they did not to recognise Him. Today, He is now as a nobleman who has gone into a far country to obtain for himself a kingdom, and to return. (See Luke 19:12.) When He returns the Lord Jesus will establish in the earth the kingdom for which all Christendom prays.

The idea of such a kingdom is so common in scripture and the references to it are so numerous, that a failure to note the different senses in which the term itself is used can only be the cause of much misunderstanding. But if we are careful to distinguish between things that differ, then all becomes plain, and absurd and foolish jibes about the Bible contradicting itself are seen for what they really are.

The kingdom is often referred to in a *providential* sense as, for instance, when we read, "The Lord has prepared His throne in the heavens, and His kingdom rules over all" (Psa.103:19). Over against that, Jesus used the same term, but in its *spiritual* sense, when He told Nicodemus, "Except a man be born of water and of the Spirit, he cannot enter into the kingdom of God" (John 3:5).

The kingdom needs to be understood in a *historical* sense as well. This takes us back to the theocratic kingdom of David and Solomon.

Saul, the first king of Israel, was told at the beginning of his reign, "The Lord anointed you king over Israel." But later, he was informed, "The Lord has rejected you from being king over Israel" (1Sam.15:17,26). Quite obviously, the direct government of God held immediate sway over the affairs of the chosen nation at that time.

Scripture also speaks of the kingdom in an *eternal* sense. And so we read, "The Lord shall reign forever and ever" (Ex.15:18). But there is a further, and, we might add, much misunderstood aspect of the kingdom. It is the kingdom in its *Messianic* sense, often referred to as our Lord's millennial reign. Nor are these last two concepts incompatible for the latter will flow out into the former like a great sea flowing out into an even greater ocean. It is the *millennial* aspect of the kingdom that is especially prominent in the servant songs.

The Kingdom of the Son of Man

To say that the messianic or millennial kingdom is one of the core themes of scripture is not to overstate the case. More than two and a half millennia have now passed since Daniel, the prophet, was given a revelation of the then future political arrangements for the earth. Great empires would hold centre stage, one succeeding another, until, when they would all have passed away, one like the Son of Man would come to receive a kingdom that would never pass away. (See Dan.2&7.) This can only be a reference to Messiah's future reign.

The Lord Jesus Himself spoke of the coming of the Son of Man to establish a kingdom in the earth. In His Olivet teaching He announced, "Immediately after the tribulation of those days shall the sun be darkened, and the moon shall not give her light, and the stars shall fall from heaven, and the powers of the heavens shall be shaken. And then shall appear the sign of the Son of Man in heaven; and then shall all the tribes of the earth mourn, and they shall see the Son of Man coming in the clouds of heaven with power and great glory" (Matt.24:29,30). Nor can there be any dispute about the identity of the Son of Man, for this title was frequently used of the Lord Jesus, during the course of His earthly ministry.

The Kingdom in History and Prophecy

The kingdom theme is also prominent in the prophecy of Zechariah. Anticipating the Lord's coming again, the prophet said, "Then shall the Lord go forth, and fight against those nations, as when He fought in the day of battle. And His feet shall stand in that day upon the mount of Olives ... and the Lord shall be king over all the earth" (Zech.14:3,4&9). Here we have the Lord engaging in certain activities in that coming day, that are reminiscent of similar activities in former days.

For instance, there are numerous examples in the sacred history of how the Lord fought for His people in actual physical battles. Take, for example, the famous occasion when triumphant Israel stood on the wilderness bank of the Red Sea, and saw the corpses of Pharaoh's military float on the surface of the water. They praised the Lord for what He had done and said, "I will sing unto the Lord, for He has triumphed gloriously: the horse and his rider has He thrown into the sea" (Ex.15:1).

The same kind of thing happened at the time of Israel's entry into Canaan, when Joshua commanded the sun to stand still. "There was no day like that before it or after it, that the Lord hearkened unto the voice of a man; for the Lord fought for Israel" (Joshua10:14). Another notable occasion was when God dramatically answered the prayer of Jehoshaphat, and destroyed the children of Ammon and of Moab, and the inhabitants of Mount Seir, who had besieged Jerusalem. The record states, "The Lord fought against the enemies of Israel" (2Chron.20:29).

In the light of these and other instances of direct supernatural intervention in human affairs, it should not be difficult to understand that Zechariah was clearly predicting similar interventions at the second advent. The language he employed is quite straightforward, the historical allusions to it are both literal and factual, and fairness requires us to understand his predictions for the future in the same way.

The Glorious Reign

The Bible testimonies to that coming kingdom, that future sabbath of rest, are too numerous to be catalogued in these pages. But here are a few references from Isaiah:

Isaiah 2:2-4

"It shall come to pass in the last days, that the mountain of the Lord's house shall be established in the top of the mountains, and shall be exalted above the hills; and all nations shall flow unto it. And many people shall go and say, Come and let us go up to the mountain of the Lord, to the house of the God of Jacob; and He will teach us of His ways, and we will walk in His paths; for out of Zion shall go forth the law, and the word of the Lord from Jerusalem. And He shall judge among the nations, and shall rebuke many peoples; and they shall beat their swords into plowshares, and their spears into pruning hooks; nation shall not lift up sword against nation, neither shall they learn war any more."

Isaiah 11:4,5,10

"But with righteousness shall He judge the poor, and reprove with equity for the meek of the earth; and He shall smite the earth with the rod of His mouth, and with the breath of His lips shall He slay the wicked. And righteousness shall be the girdle of His loins, and faithfulness the girdle of His waist. In that day there shall be a root of Jesse, who shall stand for an ensign of the people; to Him shall the nations seek, and His rest shall be glorious."

Isaiah 32:1,16,17

"Behold, a king shall reign in righteousness, and princes shall rule in judgement. Then judgement shall dwell in the wilderness, and righteousness remain in the fruitful field. And the work of righteousness shall be peace; and the effect of righteousness, quietness and assurance forever."

These references are taken only from the writings of a single prophet, and are just a few selected from a great number of similar allusions to the future kingdom. In addition, and probably without exception, all the prophets add their witness to Messiah's coming reign. Micah reiterated Isaiah's first reference and amplified it. (See Micah 4:3.) Jeremiah predicted, "A king shall reign and prosper, and shall execute judgement and justice in the earth" (Jer.23:5).

Zechariah also declared, "The Lord shall be King over all the earth" (Zech.14:9). And again, "He shall speak peace unto the nations; and His dominion shall be from sea even to sea, and from the river even to the ends of the earth" (Zech.9:10). And all this is in perfect accord with the central petition in the Lord's prayer; *Thy kingdom come. Thy will be done in earth, as it is in heaven* (Matt.6:10). Here we have a parallelism, the second arm of which explains or amplifies the first. The second arm says, *Thy will be done in earth, as it is in heaven.* The kingdom for which we pray envisages a universal rule of righteousness and of peace, and God's will being done in the earth.

When Jesus is King

We must never forget that the foundations of this future kingdom are already in place, having been laid in the events of Messiah's first advent. At His first coming the Lord Jesus dealt with sin and death; He destroyed him that had the power of death. And when He comes again He will come in power and great glory to reign as King of kings, and Lord of lords. Having appeared once, in lowliness and poverty, as a man of sorrows, He will then be revealed in His beauty as the man of God's right hand.

In that day three surpassing developments will combine to radically alter the entire world scene. First, accompaning the inauguration of the kingdom there will be an unprecedented and gracious outpouring of God's Spirit upon all flesh. Secondly, the deceiver of the nations, that old serpent called the Devil and Satan, will be bound. And, in the third place, the curse that was imposed at the time of the fall, will be very largely lifted from the brow of mankind.

The predominant goal of the second advent, therefore, will be the throne of glory rather than the cross of shame. Its aim will be administration rather than atonement. With trumpet sound the advent will proclaim the crowning day and the establishment of the long anticipated messianic reign. The Prince of Peace will sit upon the throne of His glory, and "in His days shall the righteous flourish, and abundance of peace so long as the moon endures" (Psa.72:7).

Isaiah gives us a fine analysis of the moral conditions of that coming day by raising this searching question, "Who among us shall dwell with the devouring fire?" This is evidently a reference to the presence of the Lord among His people in the kingdom. Here is the immediate and ready response, "He that walks righteously, and speaks uprightly; he that despises the gain of oppressions, that restrains his hands from holding bribes, that stops his ears from hearing of blood, and shuts his eyes from seeing evil; He shall dwell on high: his place of defence shall be the munitions of the rocks: bread shall be given him; his waters shall be sure" (Isa.33:14-16).

Ever since the catastrophe of the fall and perhaps especially since the flood, when the government of the earth was committed into human hands, the story has been essentially one of revolt against God, of oppression and greed and corruption. The vital difference, however, between the future kingdom age and the present time will be that the government of God will directly rule in the affairs of men. When that time comes all God's foreordained purposes, the purposes that lay behind the incarnation, will come to maturity and reach their climax. *Silvester Horne* had this future kingdom in mind when he wrote,

All men shall dwell in His marvellous light,
Races long severed His love shall unite,
Justice and truth from His sceptre shall spring,
Wrong shall be ended when Jesus is king.

The *First Song*

The Messianic Kingdom (Contd.)

He Shall Bring Forth Justice (ii)

When self-seeking statesmen or would-be dictators bring the nations to the brink of war, as they sometimes do, we should not be despairing. On the contrary, we should keep before us the awe inspiring vision that one day the nations themselves will be brought into an environment of peace and tranquillity. The unambiguous testimony of scripture is that a lasting state of justice and peace throughout the earth will be ushered in when Isaiah's Servant returns in kingly power, and *Israel's King shall reign victorious.*

That there is need for a righteous order to prevail in human affairs does not need to be argued. A moment's reflection on the state of society will be enough to impress upon us a depressing and, an ever increasing display of what the apostle Peter called, "the corruption that is in the world through lust" (2Pet.1:4). Of old it was said, "A man was famous according as he had lifted up axes upon the thick trees. But now they break down the carved work thereof at once with axes and hammers" (Psa.74:5,6). And yet, the appalling turmoil that marks our supposedly sophisticated society is only a harbinger of the lawlessness that will mark the last days.

However much we may attempt to soften it, the fact remains that the mainstream of human endeavour has been posioned by sin. This basic premise shows itself in ways without number, not least, in what the poet Burns called *man's inhumanity to man*. And then, when evil breaks out into open violence the cry goes up for peace with justice. But even in the most ordered communities this ideal, at its best, is only a relative concept. Not until Jesus comes again will such an ideal be realised in any truly meaningful sense.

The Last Days

The prophetic scriptures reveal a rather grim prospect for the time immediately prior to the second advent. The period is variously spoken of as the great tribulation, the end time or the last days. It will be marked by a strident and cynical departure from the well proven and commomly accepted standards of morality that have served us so well in the past and, like cement, have held human society together. The present, high-profile erosion of those principles is to be mourned, for while they did not cure society's ills, they had at least the merit of arresting them and slowing down society's drift towards its own destruction.

"The mystery of iniquity is already at work," warned Paul (2Thess.2:7). And it will continue until it reaches its high water mark in the lawlessness of the end time. Even casual observers of trends in today's world are able to see this insidious principle of evil rapidly and openly advancing, and in many instances, its manifestations have already reached alarming proportions.

Far from the optimistic doctrine that things are getting better, admittedly more muted now than a few years ago, the unfolding moral drama is of standards being on a steep downward spiral. It is no longer a cliche to say that the problems facing human society are almost beyond man's capacity to control them. This unpleasant fact, constantly pressed upon us from every quarter, will issue in the appearing of *the lawless one, the man of sin*, frequently referred to simply as the Antichrist.

The Man of Sin

That *man of sin*, when he appears, will be the very personification of evil in the earth. Satan will give him his power, and his throne, and great authority. (See Rev.13:1,2.) For all that, his ultimate doom is certain and his judgement sure, and we also know that his time will be short. His destruction will be brought about by the appearing in glory of the Lord Jesus at the time of His second advent. (See 2 Thess.2:8.)

Our first song, however, looks beyond these portentous events and envisages a kingdom of peace. A kingdom of universal proportions, and established on principles of righteousness. That kingdom will be instituted, not by political or religious initiatives or compromises, but by the appearing again of Jesus Christ, our Servant-King. Since the fall of our first parents in Eden's primal hour, every honest heart has been pining, whether knowingly or not, for the dawn of that glorious day when -

"Jesus shall reign where'er the sun,
Does its successive journeys run.
His kingdom stretch from shore,
Till moons shall wax and wane no more."

The Administration of the Kingdom

The scriptures quoted in our last chapter affirm the certainty of these things and make plain the radical character of Christ's coming dominion. The nature, polity and organisation of the future kingdom, will only be seen in the unique circumstances in which it will arise, as well as in the kind of principles by which it will be governed.

Governments today rule by what they know, and their knowledge is gleaned from what they hear and what they see. But their knowledge at best is limited and so their burgeoning legislation is subject to constant correction and revision. But when Jesus is King, "He shall not judge after the sight of His eyes, neither reprove after the hearing of His ears" (Isa.11:3). Since He knows the end from the beginning, it follows that His knowledge will be complete and His judgements perfect.

The repeated reference in the first song to *justice* in the earth, therefore, is full of meaning. The term itself is a legal one and we have already briefly touched on its significance. In the first instance, it stands for truth in an objective sense, and then for that same truth expressed practically in a just order. It is used in a wide variety of senses, all of them related to the many and diverse processes of governmental administration.

Scripture amply reveals how this projected justice will be administered. Visualising God standing in the congregation and among the judges, (*a.v.gods*) the psalmist called to Him, and said, "Arise, O God, judge the earth; for you shall inherit all nations" (Psa.82:8). The need for such a divine intervention is then bluntly stated. Of the perpetrators of injustice in the earth he asked, "How long will you judge unjustly, and accept the persons of the wicked? Defend the poor and fatherless; do justice to the poor and needy ... " (Psa.82:2-5).

The Psalmist's plea will be effectively answered when earth's rightful king returns, for through His anointed king God will bring forth justice in truth. "He has appointed a day, in which He will judge the world in righteousness by that man whom He has ordained" (Acts17:31). In that day every form of tyranny will be broken, and the oppressed set free. In all probability, we have a foreview of these things in Solomon's adminstration of the theocratic kingdom over which he reigned. (See 1 Kings 4.)

In addition, we should keep in mind what Jesus told the disciples. "Verily I say unto you that you who have followed me, in the regeneration, when the Son of man shall sit on the throne of His glory, you also shall sit upon twelve thrones, judging the twelve tribes of Israel" (Matt.19:28). From this it would appear that the apostles will preside over the administration of the kingdom, probably after the pattern of the theocratic judgeship that followed the death of Joshua. (See Judges 2:18.) And then, of course, we also have Paul's challenging word to Timothy concerning the believers of this age, "If we suffer, we shall also reign with Him" (2Tim.2:12).

The Original Promise

The rather startling thing is that all these things will be accomplished by our Servant-King in a way that today's statesmen, for their own very good reasons of course, would not even take into their reckoning. Following the scattering of the nations at the tower of Babel, God called Abraham out of the the land of Mesopotamia, and promised to make of him a great nation. The promise to Abraham was quite specific, "In thee shall all families of the earth be blessed" (Gen.12:2,3).

As well as being specific the promise was also confirmed, and confirmed so repeatedly, that had the difficulties of Abraham's life not required it, it would seem almost monotonous. When Abraham reached the land of Caanan the promise was immediately validated, as it was again on the occasion of his parting from Lot.

And there were other occasions as well, such as on the eve of the destruction of Sodom. At that time the Lord said, "Abraham shall surely become a great and mighty nation, and all the nations of the earth shall be blessed in him" (Gen.18:18). The pledge was also an integral part of the everlasting covenant that God made with Abraham.

This covenant promise to Abraham is tremendously significant. It is not overstating the case to say that it is one of the great keys of history, and it is the initial impulse to the eventual establishment of the future kingdom. Moreover, the promise holds to this day and in faithfulness to it, God will presently bring national Israel to a place of repentance and faith. And then, through the restored nation He will bring His peace to all the nations. But the detail of this belongs to later chapter, in fact, it is the specific theme of the next song.

The *First Song*

The Messianic Kingdom (Contd.)

He Shall Bring Forth Justice (iii)

Principles of the future kingdom

The ethical principles of the future kingdom were clearly set forth in our Lord's public ministry, and most notably, in the *sermon on the mount.* Let no one rob us of *the sermon on the mount* by telling us that it is not for our day. It must be for our day, because all scripture is given by inspiration of God and is profitable. And since divine principles transcend all dispensational divisions the principles of the sermon on the mount must be of universal application.

At the same time, however, we should recognise that *the sermon on the mount,* in its primary interpretation, anticipates the coming kingdom. The sermon is the King's manifesto and it becomes all the more interesting when we read it as such. If we can keep in mind the difference between interpretation, and application, we will be preserved from the absurd charge that a dispensational view of scripture will inevitably lead us to an antinomian position.

Having said that, we learn from the first servant song that the principles of the coming kingdom, as well as being elucidated in His oral ministry, were also enshrined in our Lord's personal life. Those moral features, so beautifully exemplified during the time of His humiliation, are an objective expression of the core principles that will govern the kingdom in the day of His glory.

And herein lies a rule of thumb, just as true for us today as it will be for others in the future. Besides having communicated His mind to us in written precepts, the living God has done this in an objective way as well. What He desires is fully told out in the person of His Son. For this reason, as we keep our eyes on the Lord Jesus in sacred contemplation, the Holy Spirit is able to do a gracious work within us; sanctifying us and changing us, and making us more like Christ. In a similar way the future kingdom will derive its moral impulse from the character of the King's own person.

Consider then, the salient features of the Servant-King's manner of living, as they are delineated for us in this first song. All was seen by the prophet in anticipation, and now it is our privilege to see how all was realised, and to note the amazing harmony between the prediction and its fulfilment.

We will, of course, always bear in mind that if our Saviour's manner and methods seem unconventional, it is because they are so different from those of earthly potentates. Among the many things we learn as we consider the life of the Lord Jesus is that our God is a moral being, and that He has created a moral universe and established it on moral principles.

The Chief End – To Glorify God

The first song begins, "Behold my servant whom I uphold, my elect, *in whom my soul delights*." This is how God speaks of His Servant (v.1). And we seem to hear an echo of this on the three occasions during His earthly ministry, when the Father broke the silence of the heavens, and testified of Him in the language of this song, "This is my beloved Son *in whom I am well pleased*."

The Father's pleasure in that consecrated life brings to our minds the pleasure He found in creation's original vitality. Looking on that primeval scene, He said, "It is good," He went further and said, "It is very good." The heavens declare the glory of God, said the psalmist, and so did the Son throughout His pilgrimage here. And the same will be true of the coming kingdom, for its moral impetus will derive from the person of its King. In fact, the whole earth will take its character from Him, who, in the days of His flesh, pleased not Himself. As a result, the entire scene will be radically transformed.

Nor is it difficult to accept that such a transformation will be a refreshing contrast to the all-pervasive existential philosophy that permeates modern society. "Let us eat, drink and be merry for tomorrow we die," is a philosophy that leaves us incapable of making any meaningful moral choices, because it leaves us without any moral values. Apart from God we have no ultimate authority. Consequently, we are robbed of any ultimate meaning to life. When we leave the living God out of the equation, man becomes his own god. He simply pleases himself, considering himself free to do his own thing.

A New Philosophy

As the song develops, attention is called to certain negative things about the Servant: *"He shall not cry, nor lift up, nor cause His voice to be heard in the street"* (v.2). In passing we should note that the cry of verse 2 is not be confused with the cry of verse 13. The latter is the cry of His enemies, and refers to their overthrow. The former relates to His friends, and emphasises His unique humbleness, and the complete absence of any form of self-promotion.

Moreover, the expression *nor cause His voice to be heard in the street,* (v.2) should not be seen as a censure upon certain types of Christian service such as open-air preaching. In its place, and properly conducted, this service may still be an effective method of communicating the gospel. As it is used here the expression carries the idea of people quarrelling in a house, and speaking so loudly, that what is said inside can be heard in the street outside. The inference is that the Servant of our song will not call attention to Himself as that quarrelsome house does, among all the houses of the street. The Servant-King's whole philosophy of life and conduct, His entire demeanour and bearing, will be one of self-effacement.

Sin in the universe

Sin might be described as behaviour inconsistent with God's ordained standards. The first sin in the universe was the sin of pride. Lucifer, the anointed cherub who stood by the throne of God, was not content with his exalted position. He declared, "I will exalt my throne above the stars of God ... I will be like the Most High" (Isa.14:13,14). For this he was cast down from heaven to become that old serpent, the Devil and Satan.

Sin in the world

The temptation of our first parents was of a similar order and had a similar result. They fell from their lofty position at the apex of creation, where all things had been subjected to them. The serpent, challenged the woman to disobey God, promising her, "You shall be as God" (Gen.3:5). Eve, in turn, involved Adam in the act of disobedience, and the resultant injury remains with us to this day. "By one man's disobedience many were made sinners" (Rom.5:19).

The same arrogant pride was seen in Nebuchadnezzar who boasted, "Is not this great Babylon, that I have built ... by the might of my power, and for the honour of my majesty?" He only learned the folly of his boastful spirit after seven years, during which he ate grass like the wild oxen. (See Dan. 4:30.)

Foolish Pride Eclipsed

The bearing of earthly kings has always been marked by pomp and ceremony and great ostentation. But our Servant-King, in His journey through this world, stood in marked contrast to every form of outward show. When riding in triumph into Jerusalem He did so "lowly and riding upon an ass" (Zech.9:9). In the most absolute sense of the term, He was "meek and lowly in heart" (Matt 11:29).

We need only reflect upon the circumstances surrounding His time among men. Nazareth, where He was brought up, was not the charming village that sentiment sometimes paints. As for the circumstances of His birth and of His baptism, both events combined to anticipate a life and a ministry free from ostentation and foolish pride. He did at times address great multitudes, but His most satisfying work was done in private, in conversation with individuals or small groups of people.

He charged the newly cleansed leper, "See you say nothing to any man" (Mk.1:44). And those who would have proclaimed His deity were forbidden to do so. Often He would withdraw from the throng, and seek privacy rather than publicity. He moved among men in a thoroughly unobtrusive manner. Of course, human nature loves to be noticed; but the true Servant of Jehovah was clothed with humility. In the same way the messianic kingdom will be marked by an absence of paltry ostentation, of arrogance and foolish pride.

A New Integrity

Character and transparency will be reinstated in the kingdom age. "The vile person shall be no more called liberal, nor the churl said to be bountiful" (Isa.32:5). "The lofty looks of man shall be humbled, and the haughtiness of men shall be bowed down, and the Lord alone shall be exalted in that day" (Isa.2:11). In similar fashion Zephaniah prophesied of that time and said, "The remnant of Israel shall not do iniquity, nor speak lies; neither shall a deceitful tongue be found in their mouth: for they shall feed and lie down, and none shall make them afraid" (Zeph.3:13).

And in the penultimate prophecy, Zechariah declared, "Everyone that is left of all the nations shall even go up from year to year to worship the King, the Lord of hosts, and to keep the feast of tabernacles. And it shall be that whoever will not come up of all the families of the earth unto Jerusalem to worship the King, the Lord of hosts, even upon them shall be no rain" (Zech.14:16,17). The clear inference is that the fear of God will be universal, and even if the submission of some is only feigned, His authority will be recognised by all, from the least to the greatest.

By putting these things in negative terms (the negative occurs six times in the first four verses), Isaiah uses a form of speech that serves to emphasise the unique grandeur of both the Servant's ministry and His peerless character. Of course, all these negatives have their echo in the opening beatitude of our Lord's *sermon on the mount*, "Blessed are the poor in spirit; for theirs is the kingdom of heaven" (Matt.5:3).

A New Civility

Many a sorely wounded spirit has found solace, in what is next said of the perfect Servant, *"a bruised reed shall He not break, and the smoking flax shall He not quench"* (v.4). All is not well with a bruised reed or with a smoking flax, and yet, the remedy lies neither with the one nor the other, it lies in the tender care which is able to effect recovery and restoration. The vital thing is not the condition of the reed or the flax, but rather, what the touch of a loving hand can do.

It may be that the reference to *a reed* alludes to a musical instrument, such as a pipe. Should the pipe become damaged, discord will result. Our Servant-King's goal is always to take away the discord from lives that have been battered and bruised by sin, and to replace it with the music of heaven.

A bruised reed is a reed that is injured but not broken; a smoking flax, or wick, is a wick that is ignited but not flaming, and both need to be handled with great care. The figures used here give us beautiful and unmistakable testimonies to the gentleness and tenderness of Christ.

The Gentleness of Christ

Isaiah witnessed to the gentleness of Christ in an earlier prophecy, "He shall feed His flock like a shepherd; He shall gather the lambs with His arm, and carry them in His bosom, and shall gently lead those that are with young" (Isa.40:11). In this song, although a different figure is used, the same feature is emphasised. And here again we seem to detect overtones of *the sermon on the mount*, for in another beatitude Jesus said, "Blessed are the merciful; for they shall obtain mercy" (Matt.5:7).

The Lord Jesus exemplified all these things in His own personal attitudes, and in His teaching He ever sought to induce a compassionate regard for the needy. He said, "Give to him who asks of you, and from him who would borrow of you turn not away" (Matt.5:42). With these features permeating the future kingdom, the result will be a complete readjustment of moral values throughout society.

We must never forget that these same principles are enjoined upon us in this Church age as well. How apt was the servant ideal Paul set before Timothy, "the servant of the Lord must not strive, but be gentle unto all" (2Tim.2:24). Too often within the household of faith, needless hurt has been sustained by sensitive souls, at the hands of their fellow-believers. We all need to be more careful to reflect the manners of the perfect Servant, in our dealings with others.

A New Economy

From the beginning it was God's intention that man should not be idle. Adam had work to do in Eden even before the fall. And after the fall, his work was greatly intensified. In today's world the issue of unemployment has been an unhappy symptom of an even deeper malaise in human society. Avoiding high inflation, while trying to generate full employment, is the vexed problem confronting every sophisticated economy. And a satisfactory solution to this issue still eludes us.

But in the coming kingdom the enigma will be solved. Zechariah declared, "For before these days there was no hire for man, nor any hire for beast; neither was there any peace to him that went out or came in because of the affliction; for I set all men, every one, against his neighbour. But now I will not be unto the residue of this people as in former days, saith the Lord of Hosts. For the seed shall be prosperous; the vine shall give its fruit, and the ground shall give its increase, and the heavens shall give their dew; and I will cause the remnant of this people to possess all these things" (Zech.8:10-12).

In these verses, the prophet seems to envision that prior to the establishment of the messianic kingdom there will be widespread unemployment in the earth. And like so many of the problems that men grapple with today, this one too, will emerge in an even more acute form in the last days. The problem will be of such an intense character, society's political leaders will have no power to relieve it. But the return of Christ the King, and the bringing in of the messianic kingdom, will introduce a new and prosperous dynamic into the situation.

A Different Value System

In that day labour will acquire a new dignity, and a true balance will be achieved between the various branches of society. Material things will no longer be the all-consuming passion that they are today. What will men not do in their lust to accumulate material possessions? But in that day they will learn to seek first the kingdom of God and His righteousness, as they are instructed to do in *the sermon on the mount*. And they will do so, confident that every needful thing will be added unto them. (See Matt.6:33.)

A Wholly New Environment

Another insight into the character of our Servant-King is given in the words, *"He shall not fail nor be discouraged"* (v.4). The word translated *'fail'* means to burn low, like a flickering candle or a lamp that is about to go out. In this, the Servant-King stands in contrast to the smoking flax of the previous verse. We are the smoking flax; 'our love is often low, our joy still ebbs and flows.' But whatever failure there may be in us, there is no failure in Him; He shall never burn low.

In addition, we read, "*He shall not be discouraged"* (*margin,* broken). Again, this contrasts with the bruised reed of the previous verse (Isa.42:3,4). We are the bruised reed, failure and breakdown are always with us, but He shall not fail. He was exposed to all the pressures, both physical and psychological, that press upon us, and He proved Himself in all the circumstances of life.

The physical well-being of the human race will be dramatically improved in the period of the messianic kingdom. For while there will be death, longevity will be greatly expanded. "Thus saith the Lord; I am returned unto Zion, and will dwell in the midst of Jerusalem: and Jerusalem shall be called a city of truth ... There shall yet old men and old women dwell in the streets of Jerusalem ... And the streets of the city shall be full of boys and girls playing in the streets thereof" (Zech.8:3-5).

"There shall be no more an infant of days, nor an old man that has not filled his days; for the child shall die an hundred years old, but the sinner, being an hundred years old, shall be accursed." A man of a hundred years will still be considered a child, while one dying young, shall be seen to be cut off for his sin. In that day "They shall build houses, and inhabit them; and they shall plant vineyards, and eat the fruit of them ... They shall not labour in vain, nor bring forth for trouble" (Isa.65:20-23).

The Animal Creation

A vital factor in the kingdom age will be the easing of the consequences of the fall. This will have a profound impact upon the entire physical creation. Human propensities towards wrong will be altered, and the wild and ferocious instincts of the animal creation will be tempered and restrained. All cause of fear, either from man or beast, will be removed, and every man will dwell safely under his vine and under his fig tree.

"The wolf also shall dwell with the lamb, and the leopard shall lie down with the kid; and the calf and the young lion and the fatling together, and a little child shall lead them. And the nursing child shall play on the hole of the asp, and the weaned child shall put his hand on the adder's den.They shall not hurt nor destroy in all my holy mountain; for the earth shall be full of the knowledge of the Lord, as the waters cover the sea" (Isa.11:6-9).

After His baptism the Lord Jesus was with the wild beasts in the wilderness for forty days, yet no harm came to Him. It was as though those wild beasts were somehow able to recognise that they were in the presence of the Lord of creation. Again, one week before His crucifixion, He rode into Jerusalem on a colt on which no one had ever sat. That, as yet unbroken, animal seemingly sensed that it was under the control of creation's Lord, and it meekly bore Him on His way. Could it be that in these and other similar events we have brief foreshadowings of millennial times?

Some might contend, no doubt with a degree of cynicism, that a kingdom established upon such principles could not survive. But this criticism is admissible only if we judge the future in the light of the present and, at the same time, set aside a number of extremely potent factors. For instance, as already pointed out, the deceiver of the nations will be bound (Rev.20:1-3). And, in part at any rate, the curse that settled upon the whole creation at the time of the fall will be lifted. Above all, God's anointed king will be upon the throne, and, "with righteousness shall He judge the poor, and reprove with equity for the meek of the earth." (See Isa.11:1-10.)

The contemplation of Christ is a sure resource from which we are able to derive strength and encouragement in our times of need. Since He is touched with the feeling of our infirmities, we can count upon Him, to minister to us timely and sufficient grace. And this especially true in those times when we are most conscious of being like the bruised reed, or the smoking flax. A similar renewing and restoring of His amazing grace will give a constant dynamic to the coming kingdom.

All shall be well in His kingdom of peace,
Freedom shall flourish and wisdom increase,
Foe shall be friend when His trimuph we sing,
Sword shall be sickle when Jesus is king.

The *First Song*

The Nations in the Kingdom

The Isles shall wait for His law (i)

Anyone bold enough to undertake a detailed study of the nations from the perspective of biblical prophecy will surely be richly rewarded. While the nations are chronicled throughout history, they are especially featured with reference to its beginning and its end.

Evidently the nations will play a large part in the many issues connected with the Lord's return, and the bringing in of the messianic kingdom. The prophet's mention of the nations in this song, therefore, is very important and should not be overlooked.

Nationhood derives from God, and the rise and fall of nations is known to Him. He has set their bounds that they cannot pass. He has also decreed that, in the end, the nations will be brought into a right relationship with Himself, and into the enjoyment of the millennial kingdom. We read that "the nations of them who are saved shall walk in the light of it, and the kings of the earth do bring their glory and honour into it ... And they shall bring the glory and honour of the nations into it" (Rev.21:24,26).

Edom

An example of this is the nation of Edom which sprang from Esau, who was called 'that profane person' and whose descendants consistently set themselves to oppose Israel. Edom appears many times in the prophetic writings and especially in the book of Obadiah. That prophet calls attention both to the nature of Edom's sin and to the justice of God's judgement. Yet the prophet's final word predicts the coming kingdom of Messiah and anticipates the raising up of saviours and of salvation for Edom.

Syria and Egypt

Damascus, the capital city of Syria, and perhaps the oldest city in the world next to Jericho, is foreseen to have a peaceful border with Israel in millennial times. (See Ezk.47:16-18.) And Egypt, Israel's traditional enemy on her southern flank, will also share in the peace and tranquility of the coming kingdom. "In that day shall Israel be the third with Egypt and with Assyria, even a blessing in the midst of the land. Whom the Lord of hosts shall bless, saying, Blessed be Egypt, my people, and Assyria, the work of my hands, and Israel, my inheritance" (Isa.19:24,25).

That this ideal of peace allied to justice is a long way removed from the present troubled state of the nations cannot be questioned, and yet nothing can invalidate the promises of God. This highly prized and much sought after objective, the family of nations being at peace with itself, and with God, will not be achieved by human diplomacy, or social expediency, or even by the clash of weaponry, however sophisticated. It will remain an illusory dream until the appearing again of God's perfect Servant, earth's rightful king. (See Isa.42:1.)

The Nations - A Brief History

The book of Genesis, the book of origins, records in considerable detail the origin of the nations. (See Genesis chapters10 &11.) After the great flood, men began again to multiply on the earth. With the passing of time, the descendants of the three sons of Noah, who survived the flood, increased by their families. Later, the various groups of families developed into nations. And at that time a single language prevailed among them.

But from the beginning those nations lapsed into many and varied forms of idolatry which provoked the living God to anger. When

God eventually moved against them, He confused their language and scattered them upon the face of the earth. Diversity of tongues and division of lands followed, and in this way each nation developed its own separate identity.

The quite remarkable thing about God's dealings with the various families that populated the earth was that the nation of Israel, as yet unformed, was always in His mind. Israel was His yardstick when He measured to the nations their territories. "When the Most High divided to the nations their inheritance, when He separated the sons of Adam, He set the bounds of the people according to the number of the children of Israel" (Deut. 32:8).

The Hebrew Race

The Old Testament is sometimes thought to be the history of the human race, but apart from the first eleven chapters, that is not so. From Genesis chapter 12 forward, the scriptures are the record of God's dealings with the new nation that sprang from Abraham; the people "of whom, as concerning the flesh, Christ came" (Rom.9:5). It is true that many other nations, some friendly and some hostile, feature in the record, but they do so only to the degree that their history impinged upon the history of Israel.

Of course, there were exceptions to this rule. And there were times when the Hebrew prophets reprimanded some of the surrounding nations because of their sinful ways. The reason they did this was that before the call of Abraham, the Lord had established certain decrees which were universal in their application. And the prophets considered it their duty to warn the nations that God would punish them for transgressing those moral standards.

Those instances apart, however, the burden of the Old Testament scriptures is God's purpose for the chosen nation, the nation of Israel. And what gives the references to the nations in this first song their special significance, is that they are grounded in the original pledge God gave to Abraham: '*in thee shall all families of the earth be blessed*' (Gen.12:3).

At the beginning there were fifty eight basic nations. Others were added later, such as the Edomites, the Ammonites and the Moabites.

But the most notable addition to the family of nations followed the call of Abraham. Called from a world of idolatry in Mesopotamia, God promised to make of Abraham's seed a great nation. When eventually that new nation appeared, it was the nation of Israel. The most reasonable point at which to ascribe nationhood to Abraham's seed, would seem to be when they came to Sinai following the Exodus from Egypt, because it was at that point they received their law.

Israel's Land

Moses led Abraham's seed out of Egypt and across the desert. But it was Joshua who brought them into Canaan. In three dazzling campaigns they subdued their enemies and took possession of the promised inheritance. The Amorite nations who were in possession of the land at that time had given themselves over to their wicked ways. And in keeping with His promise to Abraham some four hundred years earlier, God used Israel, as a scourge, to judge those nations for their wickedness. (See Gen.15:16.)

It is interesting to discover that, later, when Israel departed from the Lord and lapsed into evil ways of their own, the tables were turned, and those same Amorite nations became a scourge to chasten Israel. The book of Judges is the record of these things. In all this the Lord demonstrated His sovereignty over the nations and showed that His kingdom rules over all. He proved that He "is able to do according to His will in the army of heaven, and among the inhabitants of the earth, and none can stay His hand" (Dan.4:35).

Passing over several long periods of varied and fascinating history we come to the theocratic kingdom of David and Solomon. Once the envy of the nations, it came to an inglorious end in the days of Zedekiah, who was the last in a long line of kings to occupy the throne of David in Jerusalem. In his days Nebuchadnezzar, the all-conquering king of Babylon, laid seige against Jerusalem and overcame it. He plundered the city and laid it waste. He even destroyed the temple, and carried Zedekiah to Babylon in chains.

The Times of the Gentiles

This opened up an entirely new era in the government of the earth. '*The Times of the Gentiles*' had begun. By this expression we mean the period of Gentile dominance, or of Gentile ascendancy in the diverse political arrangements of the earth. This most significant prophetic period is still running its course, and will continue to do so until the second advent. Some awareness of the *'Times of the Gentiles'* is crucial, both in reading and in attempting to understand the prophetic scriptures.

This fitful epoch of Gentile overlordship in human affairs has already witnessed four major attempts to unite the nations. All were made independently of God, and all have come to naught. The first and greatest of these attempts at international union was made by the Babylonians under Nebuchadnezzar. Another was made by the Medes and Persians under Darius and Cyrus. After that came the Grecians, who tried the same thing under Alexander the Great and then, finally, came the Romans, who sought to achieve this elusive goal under the Caesars. But all these efforts to secure a politically unified world, while promising success, ended in failure.

The thoughtful reader will recognise in these strivings after some kind of political consensus among the nations, a pertinent witness to the inspiration of the prophetic word. For each of them in turn was in complete accord with the revelation given to the prophet Daniel. (See Daniel chapters 2&7.) The prophet had foreseen that four great powers, beginning with Babylon and ending with Rome, would successively hold centre-stage during the period of the *'Times of the Gentiles'*. He also anticipated that Rome would decline and for a while disappear, before finally re-emerging in the last days in a clearly identifiable form.

The Nations Today

The European Union

During the many centuries that followed the dissolution of the ancient Roman empire, several proposals were put forward to bring the diverse states of Europe together again into some kind of politcal and economic union. But the various nation-states persisted in doing their own things and going their own ways. After the Second World War, however, the near collapse of Europe's economic reserves, coupled with the advance of communism in the east, had the effect of reviving interest in the idea of a United States of Europe.

Over a period of some years various supranational organisations were brought into being, and a number of conventions signed, and so the concept of European Union developed. The initial moves were made hesitatingly, but gradually they gathered a momentum of their own, until a point was reached where it was found expedient that the arrangements be placed on a more formal footing. Things were brought to a head by the representatives of six European governments, at a meeting in Messina, Sicily, in June 1955.

Then in March 1957 the treaty of Rome was signed, and at that point the European Economic Comunity, usually referred to at the time as the Common Market, became a reality. Since then the process has been refined and dramatically extended until it is now impacting almost every household in Western Europe and many beyond. We cannot any longer think of these things in the abstract or as being distant and remote from ourselves, the reality is that they are already powerfully interacting upon every aspect of our lives.

But even before the Second World War had come to an end, moves were being made behind the scenes, aimed at bringing together the hitherto warring states of Western Europe. The war itself ended with the emergence of two superpowers: the United States of America in the west, and the Soviet Union in the east. This, in turn, gave rise to what became known as the Cold War, as the two superpowers held one another in tension, and for more than a generation confronted each other across the continent of Europe.

In spite of that, the nations of Western Europe persevered in their goal and have now largely grouped themselves into a single economic, cultural and political alliance. While we stop short of saying that the re-appearance of the Roman Empire is taking place before our eyes, we cannot but wonder if the present alignment of the nations, especially those of Western Europe, is not at least preparing the way for just such a development. Already, and for the first time since the fall of the Roman Empire, Europe now has its own single currency.

There are many political leaders, in all the nations that are involved, who would like to slow down this apparent drive towards a European superstate. And some, if they could, would even stop it altogether. Their principal concern may be a reluctance to face up to the loss of national sovereignty. But, like a giant juggernaut, the process just keeps rolling on and on, and its pace seems to accelerate with every passing year.

Many informed and objective observers are quite convinced that what the ancient Romans tried under the Caesars, is being tried again in our day. To many the present grouping of nations, especially the nations which are bound together by the Treaty of Rome, is simply a prelude to such a development. What we can assert with confidence, however, is that the old Roman empire will eventually be revived, and that like all the empires that have gone before, it too will come under the judgement of God, and be destroyed.

The Age of Gold

Throughout the long story of the present Christian era, the labours of high minded statesmen to bring harmony to the nations, and to establish some sort of lasting peace and tranquillity upon the earth, have similarly come to nothing. The scripture still holds true which says "the nations are like the troubled sea" (Isa.57:20). But all is not gloom and doom, for the theme of the first song is that better things are purposed for the family of nations.

God's declared intention is to *bring forth justice to the nations* (Isa.42:3). The verb used here denotes something that will be revealed when the time comes, rather than something that will be progressively established after repeated failed attempts. 'Peace on earth' was pledged through the lips of angels at the first advent; it will be established at the second.

When earth is finally brought into harmony with heaven, and the will of God is done on earth as it is in heaven, what we might term the capstone of prophecy will then be put in place. The messianic kingdom will be established. Isaiah declared of that time, "The glory of the Lord shall be revealed, and all flesh shall see it together" (Isa.40:5). And, again, "The Lord has made bare His holy arm in the eyes of all the nations; and all the ends of the earth shall see the salvation of our God" (Isa.52:10).

I cannot tell how He will win the nations,
How He will claim His earthly heritage,
How satisfy the needs and aspirations
Of east and west, of sinner and of sage.
But this I know, all flesh shall see His glory,
And He shall reap the harvest he has sown,
And some glad day His sun shall shine in splendour
When He the Saviour, Saviour of the world, is known.

I cannot tell how all the lands shall worship,
When, at His bidding, every storm is stilled,
Or who can say how great the jubilation
When all the hearts of men with love are filled.
But this I know, the skies will thrill with rapture,
And myriad, myriad human voices sing,
And earth to heaven, and heaven to earth, will answer:
At last the Saviour, Saviour of the world, is King!

W.Y.Fullerton.

The *First Song*

The Nations in the Kingdom (Contd.)

The Isles shall wait for His law (ii)

The Revealed Order

The order in which these things will come to pass is carefully detailed for us in the scriptures. In a notable passage on the end time, Matthew records how Jesus foretold His coming again, and the setting up of His earthly kingdom. "When the Son of man shall come in His glory, and all the holy angels with Him, then shall He sit upon the throne of His glory, and *before Him shall be gathered all nations;* and He shall separate them one from another, as a shepherd divides his sheep from the goats. And He shall set the sheep on His right hand, but the goats on His left" (Matt. 25:31-34).

It is difficult to avoid the conclusion that this a judgement of nations as nations. Whatever individual judging there might be, the fact remains that at the Lord's return, there will be a dividing of *the nations, as nations*. They will be divided into the sheep nations on His right hand, and the goat nations on His left. This judgement is different in several essentials from both the Judgement Seat [or Bema] of Christ, and the judgement of the Great White Throne.

The book of Revelation spells these things out in their sequential stages. The second advent, when the nations will be judged, is before us in the closing verses of chapter 19. The following chapter introduces us to the one thousand year reign of Christ. This sequence of events is continued in chapter 21, where the glory of the one thousand year period is deftly sketched. Admittedly, some of the imagery may be thought difficult, but much of it is plain enough for us to understand.

These concluding chapters of the Bible disclose that at the beginning of the millennial reign 'the deceiver of the nations' will be bound. This, in turn, will clear the way for the ideals expressed in the first Servant song to be realised. After that, and following the Great White Throne judgement, the millennial reign will flow out into the eternal state, and "The Lord shall reign for ever and ever" (Ex.15:18).

The Millennial Reign

But the millennial itself will be a determinate period within time, when the purposes of God respecting the Church, the nation of Israel and the Gentile nations, will come to their fullness. Of that coming kingdom we are told, "The nations of them who are saved shall walk in the light of it, and the kings of the earth do bring their glory and honour into it" (Rev.21:24). This reference to the nations in the messianic kingdom probably looks back to the sheep nations in the parable mentioned earlier.

A whole series of preparatory judgements are scheduled to take place at the time of the second advent. Some of them will impact the nation of Israel, either directly or indirectly, and others will be designed to subdue her enemies. Even then, many will persist in their rebellion against the God of truth, preferring to believe the Devil's lie. It would seem that all such will be purged from the earth before the kingdom is finally established. (See 2Thess.2:11,12.)

To the Thessalonian Christians who, at the time, were evidently under a great deal of pressure, Paul wrote, "You who are troubled, rest with us, [ie. together with us] when the Lord Jesus shall be revealed from heaven with His mighty angels, in flaming fire taking vengeance on them that know not God, and that obey not the gospel of our Lord Jesus Christ; who shall be punished with everlasting destruction *from* the presence of the Lord, and *from* the glory of His power" (2Thess.1:7-9).

When the earth was purged by the waters of the great flood, a saved family was preserved to enter upon the new earth. It would appear that a saved humanity likewise will enter the messianic kingdom. At its establishment its citizens will be clothed in 'garments of salvation' (Isa.61:10). This is not to deny that their offspring, during the kingdom period, will be unregenerate, and each of them will need to draw water out of the wells of Salvation. (See Isa.12:3.)

The Spirit poured forth

We have referred briefly to how the bringing in of the messianic kingdom will be accompanied by a great effusion of the Spirit of God. This will give the whole enterprise a tremendous spiritual dimension. Joel prophesied of those days, and said, "I will pour out my Spirit upon all flesh; and your sons and your daughters shall prophesy, your old men shall dream dreams, your young men shall see visions; and, also, upon the servants and upon the handmaids in those days will I pour out my Spirit" (Joel 2:28,29). This sort of thing actually took place at Pentecost, (See Acts chapter 2.) but quite clearly what happened then did not exhaust the meaning of this scripture.

Zechariah referred to this same spiritual dimension when he said, "And I will pour upon the house of David, and upon the inhabitants of Jerusalem, the Spirit of grace and of supplications; and they shall look upon me whom they have pierced, and they shall mourn for him, as one mourns for his only son, and shall be in bitterness for him, as one that is in bitterness for his firstborn" (Zech.12:10).

It will be Israel's chief glory in that day that Jerusalem once again has become the city of the Great King, and the joy of the whole earth. "Out of Zion shall go forth the law, and the word of the Lord from Jerusalem" (Micah 4:2). Not until then will the divine purpose behind the continued existence of the chosen people become plain. Abraham's seed had not been chosen to enjoy their privileges alone and in grand isolation. On the contrary, they were intended to be a beacon to the nations, instructing them, and inspiring them in the ways of Jehovah.

Clearly the day of these things is not yet, although the first flicker of the coming dawn may already be glimpsed on the distant horizon. But when it comes, as come it will, and the life of the world is governed by the law of the Lord, war and strife will give way to peace and prosperity. And the pledge of this first song will be gloriously redeemed, "He shall bring forth justice to the nations, and the isles shall wait for His law."

Meanwhile, the word of the Lord concerning the government of the nations still stands, "I will overturn, overturn, overturn ... until He comes whose right it is; and I will give it to Him" (Ezk.21:27). Babylon, Persia, Greece and Rome, in both their rise and fall, contribute their incontrovertible witness to the assertion that "Known unto God are all His works from the beginning" (Acts15:18). Napoleon and Hitler, to name but two, may have aspired to world domination, but the reality is that universal authority has been vested in only one man, the risen Lord Jesus Christ, the Servant of Isaiah's songs, who is coming back again.

"All power is given unto me,
In heaven and in earth."
(Matt.28:18)

The *First Song*

God Speaks to His Servant

Because these songs are so neatly blended into Isaiah's prophecy, it is sometimes difficult to tell at what point a given song ends and comment upon it begins. But a notable feature of the songs is that each is followed by a call to universal praise, to 'sing unto the Lord' and to raise 'the voice of melody,' etc. It is not unreasonable to assume that each song concludes precisely at the point where this summons is issued. In any case, we shall make that point our marker. The first song, therefore, reaches its close in Isaiah 42 verse 9.

The pledges already given in the first part of the song are now confirmed in its second stanza. Compare "*Behold my Servant, whom I uphold*" (v.1) with, "*I, the Lord ... will hold thine hand*" (v.6). In these verses the Servant is addressed directly; His power, His promises and His purposes are all asserted with emphasis. His immediate task in that day will be "*to open blind eyes, to bring out the prisoners ... who sit in darkness out of the prison house*" (v.7).

The opening of blind eyes may have reference to the covenant people of the previous verse. We certainly know that at present "blindness in part is happened to Israel, until the fullness of the Gentiles be come in" (Rom.11:25). In the same way 'those who sit in darkness' may parallel the Gentile nations, who are described in the previous verse as those who stand in need of light.

Only when Jesus comes in the glory of His second advent, "*for a covenant of the people, for a light of the nations*" (v.6) will these things be realised. "In that day there shall be a root of Jesse, who shall stand for an ensign of the peoples; to Him shall the the nations seek, and His rest shall be glorious … and He shall set up an ensign for the nations, and shall assemble the outcasts of Israel, and gather together the dispersed of Judah from the four corners of the earth" (Isa.11:10-12). Not until then will Isaiah's pledge be redeemed, that justice will be established in the earth and "*the isles shall wait for His law*" (Isa.42:4).

God the Creator

That all this will finally be accomplished is now placed beyond question, for it is as the creator of all things that God asserts their certainty. "*Thus says God, the Lord, He who created the heavens ...* " (v.5). The literal fact of creation is stated clearly enough in the Genesis record, but here figurative language is employed to describe how it was done. The heavens were *'stretched out'* like a marquee, and the earth was '*spread out*' as a goldsmith might beat out a strip of gold.

The prophet also declares that all the produce of the earth and every living thing in it, is derived from God, the creator. "He who created the heavens, and stretched them out; He who spread forth the earth, and that which comes out of it; He who gives breath to the people upon it, and spirit to them that walk in it" (Isa.42:5). How majestic is the scripture which says, "The earth is the Lord's, and the fullness thereof; the world, and they who dwell therein" (Psa.24:1). "He causes the grass to grow ... and herb for the service of man ... and wine ... and bread ... " (Psa.104: 14,15).

God has made known His eternal power and Godhead in the vast creation. "The heavens declare the glory of God, and the firmament shows His handiwork" (Psa.19:1). Of course, divine power has been manifested in other ways, besides its display in creation. In ancient times, God's power was thought of in terms of the power by which He brought His people out of Egypt, and guided them across the desert, eventually establishing them in Canaan.

To-day, we speak of God's power as it was displayed in the resurrection of Jesus Christ. "The exceeding greatness of His power toward us who believe, according to the working of His mighty power, which He wrought in Christ, when He raised Him from the dead, and set Him at His own right hand in the heavenly places, far above all ... " (Eph.1:19-21).

But in that day it will be spoken of as the power that has brought the remnant of Israel from the four corners of the earth and re-established them in the promised land. "Therefore, behold, the days come, saith the Lord, that it shall no more be said, The Lord liveth, who brought up the children of Israel out of the land of Egypt, but, the Lord liveth, who brought up the children of Israel from the land of the north, and from all the lands where He had driven them; and I will bring them again into their land that I gave to their fathers" (Jer.16:14,15).

So, having proclaimed the coming of Messiah and the ministry He will accomplish, the prophet boldly asserts, that since God is almighty, His competence to fulfil His purpose is absolute. He argues that all the inhabitants of the earth are as grasshoppers before Him, and that, by comparison with the Living God, the gods men worship are as nothing at all.

Someone might ask, "Why is the creation model of God's power the one used in this song?" The probable answer is that creation itself will experience a liberation at the return of Christ and the establishment of His kingdom. Until then, "the whole creation groans and travails in pain together." But when He comes, creation itself "will be delivered from the bondage of corruption into the glorious liberty of the children of God." (See Rom.8:21,22.) The argument, therefore, seems to be that what God has done before, He can, and will, do again.

What's in a Name

We might recall, before concluding this chapter, how the everlasting God made Himself known to Moses by the name *Jehovah*. (See Ex.3:14.) This is the name by which He declared the unchangeable nature of His character. The term means, *the ever existing one, the great I am*. But more than that: Jehovah was the covenant name. He entered into a covenant with the people, that they would be His people, and He would be their God. The relationship would be personal and intimate, and the pledge of this lay in the covenant name.

In this song, the repetition of that name is simply an affirmation of the integrity of God's promises. His name is the guarantee of His word. "*Thus says God, the LORD ...* " *and again, "I the LORD, have called ...* " (v.5,6). To the Servant-King the Lord gives precious promises, "*I ... will hold thine hand, and will keep thee, and give thee for a covenant of the people, for a light of the nations*" (v.6). None of these pledges can fail, for both God's name and His reputation are staked on their fulfilment.

In keeping with this our song maintains that it is the glory of God, that "*the former things are come to pass*" (v.9). It then goes on to argue that in the same way the new things here made known will also be fulfilled (v.9). The former things are those predictions that had been fulfilled up to that time; they may also include the predictions concerning the exiles' return to Zion, after their seventy years' captivity in Babylon. (See Isa.48:20.) The new things are the pledges given in this song. These new things are also impossible of failure because they are underpinned by both the name and the character of our unchangeable God (v.8).

The Promises of God

We recognise, of course, that while scripture has only one interpretation, it has many applications. And since all scripture is profitable, we must apply these things to ourselves, albeit in a secondary sense. We are certainly justified in doing so, for the Lord Jesus used similar language to encourage the apostle Paul. In fact, this is the very scripture God used to reveal to Paul the divine plan for his life, and through it Paul received his commission as the apostle to the Gentiles. (See Acts 26:18.)

Moreover, exceeding great and precious promises have been given to us as well, promises that cannot fail. We, too, have been called in righteousness, and He holds us in His hand. Even now He is making us able ministers of the new covenant, and His love will not be satisfied until we are finally presented faultless before the presence of His glory.

The character of these promises is such that each succeeding generation of believers has been able to echo the words of Joshua, “not one thing has failed of all the good things which the Lord your God spoke concerning you; all are come to pass” (Josh.23:14). However much appearances may have been against them, the godly in every age have laid hold on the promises of God, they have put their confidence in that word which is ‘forever settled in heaven’ (Psa.119:89). And trusting wholly in the God who gave the promises they have found Him wholly true.

This first song then introduces the Servant-King, and gives us an overview of His ministry. It highlights His faithfulness and anticipates the ultimate success of His mission. He will accomplish salvation and establish God’s will in the earth. In the meantime, for their fulfilment, the purposes of God must linger, and the whole creation must await the second advent. But He shall not fail, for the power by which all will be accomplished is the same power that brought creation into being at the first.

An immediate call to universal worship follows this first song of the Servant-King (v.10). And so it shall be, for when Christ is King, universal worship will be brought to Him, worship that will find its expression in the language of the eighth psalm, “O Lord, our Lord, how excellent is thy name in all the earth” (Psa.8:1). After tracing the fall and the still future rising again of Israel, Paul, the apostle, brings us to the same point and contributes his own doxology, “Oh, the depth of the riches both of the wisdom and knowledge of God! How unsearchable are His judgements, and His ways past finding out!” (Rom.11:33).

Thy kingdom come, O God; Thy rule, O Christ, begin;
Break with thine iron rod the tyrannies of sin.
O’er heathen lands afar thick darkness broodeth yet;
Arise, O Morning star, arise and never set.

1 Listen, O isles, unto me; and hearken, you peoples, from far: The Lord has called me from the womb; from the body of my mother has he made mention of my name.
2 And he has made my mouth like a sharp sword; in the shadow of his hand has he hidden me, and made me a polished shaft; in his quiver has he hidden me,
3 And said unto me, Thou art my servant, O Israel, in whom I will be glorified.
4 Then I said, I have laboured in vain, I have spent my strength for nothing, and in vain; yet surely my judgement is with the Lord, and my work with my God.
5 And now, saith the Lord who formed me from the womb to be his servant, to bring Jacob again to him, Though Israel be not gathered, yet shall I be glorious in the eyes of the Lord, and my God shall be my strength.
6 And he said, It is a light thing that you shouldest be my servant to raise up the tribes of Jacob, and to restore the preserved of Israel; I will also give you for a light to the [nations], that you may be my salvation to the ends of the earth.
7 Thus saith the Lord, the Redeemer of Israel, and his Holy One, to him whom man despiseth, to him whom the nation abhorreth, to a servant of rulers: Kings shall see and arise, princes also shall worship, because of the Lord who is faithful, and the Holy One of Israel, and he shall choose thee.
8 Thus saith the Lord: In an acceptable time have I heard you, and in a day of salvation have I helped you; and I will preserve you, and give you for a covenant of the people, to establish the earth, to cause to inherit the desolate heritages,
9 That you may say to the prisoners, Go forth; to them who are in darkness, Show yourselves. They shall feed in the ways, and their pastures shall be in all high places.
10 They shall not hunger nor thirst, neither shall the heat nor sun smite them; for he who has mercy on them shall lead them, even by the springs of water shall he guide them.
11 And I will make all my mountains a way, and my highways shall be exalted.
12 Behold, these shall come from far; and, lo, these from the north and from the west; and these from the land of Sinim.

2nd Servant Song: Isaiah 49:1-12

The *Second Song*

This song teaches that the coming messianic kingdom will be established through the prior restoration of national Israel to the Lord. At His first advent the nation refused Him, but when He comes again Israel will be regathered, and restored, and the Servant's mission will then include the bringing in of the kingdom.

The Proclamation of the Kingdom

Listen, O Isles, unto me (v.1)

The central section of the second part of Isaiah's prophecy begins with this song. Having learned of the Servant's mission to bring peace to this troubled world, our attention is now turned to the Servant Himself. We find Him deeply conscious of the difficulty of His task, He even speaks of the apparent futility of the effort, but He also testifies to the word of God that sustained Him in His distress.

The Servant as a Herald

The Servant is introduced as a Herald who claims the right to be universally heard. With clarion voice He calls to the nations, "*Listen, O isles [distant lands], unto me; and hearken you people, from far*" (v.1). He also identifies Himself as one who had been pre-natally named. "*The Lord has called me from the womb; from the body of my mother has He made mention of my name*" (v.1). In the first gospel, Matthew tells us that this claim was factually fulfilled in Jesus Christ. (See Matt.1:20,21.)

It is an interesting detail, and one we simply notice in passing, that while there are several references in the Old Testament to the human mother of Messiah, there is no reference to a human father. When the promise was given of the redeemer who would come, it was revealed that the seed of *the woman* would bruise the serpent's head. (See Gen.3:14-16.) Much later, Isaiah predicted, "Behold *a virgin* shall conceive, and shall bear a son, and shall call his name Immanuel" (Isa.7:14). And when the appointed time came the incarnate Son was conceived of the Holy Spirit and born of the virgin Mary.

The Servant's Preservation

In a double reference, this unusual herald speaks of Himself as being hidden, (i) *in the shadow of His hand*, and (ii) *in His quiver* (v.2). In the first instance, this probably refers to how the Servant was protected and preserved from the time of His birth. The Lord Jesus was the child born and the Son given. His life and death were a unique unveiling of God's wonderful love. His very presence on earth was a living expression of God's ideal for mankind. And one day the government of the whole earth will rest upon His shoulder.

But Herod, the Edomite, saw Him as a rival, and resolved to eliminate Him while still in infancy. Since Herod was the epitome of sensuality and pride, we are not at all surprised to learn that he sought to destroy the young child. In the event, Herod himself was destroyed, but Jesus is alive for evermore. "Kept from the paths of the destroyer" (Psa.17:4), is how the scripture summed up in advance, the preserving hand of God upon His Son.

Some thirty years later certain ill disposed persons, from among His own people, would have brought about His destruction by casting Him over the brow of a hill, but this was not to be. On several occasions the religious leaders of the day would have taken Him, but they were paralysed by a fear of the people. There was always a restraint upon what His foes might do. The essential reason was this, 'His hour was not yet come'. In every sense, He was immortal until God's time came, and then, when God's clock struck, He willingly yielded up His life.

The Servant's Preparation

The double reference to being hidden, however, must have had a further and fuller significance. In all its aspects, the life of the Lord Jesus during what we call the years of obscurity, was a careful preparation for the work the Father had given Him to do. It has always been God's way to prepare His servants in secret before appointing them to their ministry. And the terms used in this song clearly imply both a period and a process of preparation.

The Herald who calls upon the distant lands to listen, speaks in some detail of His own preparation. He says, "*The Lord called me ... the Lord made me ... the Lord hid me*" (Isa.49:1,2). Every syllable used here represents a great deal of soul searching in the secret place. And all is acutely heightened by the intense and personal nature of the language; *the Lord and me*. The principle of preparation for service is certainly established in these phrases. Clearly, there was a side to the perfect Servant's life that was out of sight from public view.

Two Striking Figures

Two rather striking figures are employed to describe this exercise. "*He has made my mouth like a sharp sword ... and made me a polished shaft*" (v.2). Imagine, if you can, the grinding and the honing that were involved in the *sharp sword*, and the cutting and the polishing that lay behind the *polished shaft* (v.2). Both figures are mirror images of our Saviour's inner groanings in the days of His pilgrimage.

Although He "learned obedience by the things which He suffered" (Hebs.5:8), He never needed to learn to obey, for He always was the subject one. But He did experience what obedience involved in practical terms and in a hostile scene. Passing through this vale of tears He encountered at close quarters, the suffering and affliction of His people. And that experience, as well as the many things He suffered, served to prepare Him for His present ministry as our great High Priest.

Mature believers are often heard testifying to a working of this principle in their own lives. In retrospect, they are able to look back and see that before major issues arose, the Lord had already been preparing them in other, and seemingly unrelated, circumstances. They may not even have been aware of any particular discipline at the time. But afterwards, they have been able to discern a strange working of divine providence in their affairs. They have even found events working out for their good, which at first had seemed only evil.

"With whom have you left those few sheep in the wilderness?" But David acquired a knowledge of God through what he learned in the wilderness, in the presence of the lion and the bear. And it was this knowledge of God that enabled him to stand in the presence of the uncircumcised Philistine, from whom, at the mere sound of his voice, all Israel fled in fear.

The Sharp Sword

The public profile of this Herald is very important, and the second song calls particular attention to this aspect of His ministry. The sharp sword is clearly a reference to His mouth, and in all probability, is a figure of speech for His words. "He has made my mouth like a sharp sword" (v.2). Scripture certainly uses the 'sharp sword' as a metaphor for the word of God, signifying its penetrating power. "For the word of God is living, and powerful, and sharper than any two-edged sword."(compare Hebs.4:12 and Rev.1:16.)

The Lord Jesus is properly called 'the Word of God', for He was God's mouthpiece. He could say, "the words that I speak unto you, they are spirit, and they are life." His words were words which the Father had given Him to speak. It is not surprising, therefore, that His hearers remarked, "Never man spoke like this man." (See John 7:46; 14:10; 17:8.)

Where, in any literature, is there anything to compare with the words of Jesus Christ? He did not write a book, yet 'His speech is gone out through all the earth, and His words to the end of the world.' We have no knowledge of anything He may have written, apart from an unrecorded statement he wrote one day in the dust, and yet the records of His words are marvels of literary beauty. What He said was always weighty and piercing, while at the same time and for the most part, it was plain and simple.

That single sentence, left unrecorded, was quite sufficient to silence those who demanded the stoning of an unfortunate woman, who had been taken in the act of adultery. With devastating effect He rebuked them saying, "He that is without sin among you, let him first cast a stone at her" (John 8:7). And those who would have embroiled Him in controversy over some politically sensitive matter were left speechless when He said, "Render to Caesar the things that are Caesar's, and to God the things that are God's" (Matt 22:21,22).

The Arrow in the Quiver

The arrow in the quiver is also a telling expression. Such an arrow is in the place where the marksman can easily lay his hand on it. The Lord Jesus was always there. Although He was not revealed until the appointed time, He was always available for the service of God. The apostle Peter spoke of Him as one, "Who verily was foreordained before the foundation of the world, but was manifest in these last times for you" (1Pet.1:20).

When the Father asked, "Whom shall I send?" the Son replied, "Here am I; send me" (Isa.6:8). This readiness to do the Father's will compelled Him, on one well-reported occasion, to go through Samaria. Although we know of the conversion of just one woman and a few men at that time, those few converts proved to be an earnest of the great harvest which was later reaped in that same place, through the ministry of Philip the evangelist. (See Acts 8.)

It is now our turn to occupy the place of the arrow in the marksman's quiver. 'In Christ's stead' is how Paul defined our present position (2Cor.5:20). In the work place and in the home, in the daily round and the common task, we must consider ourselves to be in Christ's stead. Our manner of living is to be an expression of Christ before those who do not yet know Him.

To be truly in Christ's stead, and to represent Him faithfully, we must cultivate a spiritual life that has its springs, in the secret place of fellowship and communion with the Lord. For when the balance sheet is finally drawn up, it shall be shown that what we really are is what we are before God, nothing more and nothing less.

The quiet time and the secret place

We must stress as a matter of cardinal importance, that every disciple of Christ should have a devotional life before God. The secret place is where God has always made ready His servants, and it is no different today. Moses is an early example of this principle. He had to unlearn the wisdom of Egypt, before he could become a suitable instrument for God to use. And it took forty lonely years in the wilderness of Midian for this to be achieved.

The same was true of David, who was a man after God's own heart. Eliab his older brother might cynically inquire, "With whom have you left those few sheep in the wilderness?" But David acquired a knowledge of God through what he learned in the wilderness, in the presence of the lion and the bear. And it was this knowledge of God that enabled him to stand in the presence of the uncircumcised Philistine, from whom, at the mere sound of his voice, all Israel fled in fear.

In like manner, while standing before the king of Israel, the prophet Elijah was able to say, "As the Lord God of Israel lives, *before whom I stand,* there shall not be dew nor rain these years, but according to my word" (1Kings.17:1). The basis of his boldness was that even as he stood before Ahab, the prophet was mindful of the higher power, and was consciously standing before the living God. Many centuries later, the apostle James called attention to this as the reason why the heavens withheld their rain when Elijah prayed (Jas.5:17,18).

It does seem that *the quiet time* and *the secret place*, once common terms in every Christian's vocabulary, are now almost wholly unfamiliar. It must be worthwhile, therefore, to pause and to ask ourselves, are these things important to us in any meaningful sense? We should examine ourselves, and prove ourselves; are we content with the time we spend before the Lord, in comparison to the time we spend at other things, such as watching television or reading newspapers? We must take seriously what Jesus said to the disciples, "Come apart … and rest awhile" (Mark 6:31). In view of the pace and stress of modern living it is all the more urgent that we regularly repair to the secret of His presence.

The *Second Song*

1. The Strategic Goal

I will be glorified (i)

The glory of God is the regulative principle of Christian living; it will regulate both what we do, and how we do it. This holds good for our personal and domestic lives, as it does also for the corporate life of the church. Our rule in all things must be, "whatever you do, do all to the glory of God" (1Cor.10:31). It is prudent, therefore, from time to time to examine what we are doing, and the way in which we are doing it, and to ask, is this consistent with the glory of God? How will this reflect on His honour, whom we profess to serve?

The force of the prophet's statement should not be missed; "*Thou art my Servant, O Israel, in whom I will be glorified*" (v.3). (The term *Israel* seems to be used here as a personal name for Messiah in the same way as it was first given as a personal name to Jacob. See also vv.5&6, where *Israel the servant* is nevertheless clearly distinguished from *Israel the nation*. In any case it will only be in association with Messiah that the restored nation will glorify God and thus fulfil its destiny.)

The Glory of God in a Human Vessel

The presence of the Lord Jesus among men meant that for the first time, there was a competent vessel on the earth, capable of displaying God's glory in all its transcendent radiance. Such is the mystery of the *Trinity*, the Son could assume our humanity, without ceasing to be God. And in doing this the Lord Jesus completely and finally made God known. Only the Lord Jesus could be the express image of God's person, for He alone was "God manifest in flesh" (1Tim.3:16).

That this was the Servant's supreme aim, to which all else was secondary, is brought into prominence in this second song. His all consuming passion was to glorify God in the very scene where God's name had been dishonoured. We often reflect on how He glorified God in His life, but this was true of His death as well. In fact, this is the core truth of the Christian gospel.

After Judas had made his exit from the upper room, the stage was set for those events to take place, which would bring greatest glory to both the Father and the Son. For God was glorified in every attribute of His being in the cross of Christ. It was there that God's love found its greatest expression, and there too, His righteous claims were fully satisfied.

Having thus glorified the Father, the Father, in turn, glorified the Son by raising Him from the dead, and by exalting Him to His own right hand, far above all principality and power. (See John 13:31,32.) In his first address to the Jews at Pentecost, Peter announced to those assembled, "God has made this same Jesus, whom you crucified, both Lord and Christ" (Acts 2:36).

And yet this exaltation of Christ is a very private matter. It is recognised in heaven and, on earth, in the hearts of those who love Him. As for the world at large; *our Lord is still rejected*. However, the day of His appearing is drawing near when His glory will be publicly revealed. In that day, every eye shall see Him, every knee shall bow before Him. We are told that even the nations will come, in silent awe, to worship at His feet.

The Dark Background

This second song enables us to see with greater brilliance the glory that shall be revealed at the time of His coming again, by reminding us of the Servant's humiliation. The prophet speaks of Him as '*one whom men despised*,' as '*one whom the nation abhorred*' and as '*a servant of rulers*' (v.7). Since 'the times of the Gentiles' had already begun, the last of these expressions may denote His complete identification with the people of Israel, who had become subservient to their Gentile overlords and were no longer independent as a nation.

On the other hand, this peculiar phrase may simply refer to how the Lord Jesus voluntarily subjected Himself to the Roman authorities so that the purpose for which He had come might be fulfilled. The apostolic band asserted that, "Both Herod and Pontius Pilate, with the Gentiles, and the people of Israel, were gathered together, to do whatever God's hand and counsel determined before to be done" (Acts 4:27,28).

In keeping with this, when Pilate boasted in the judgement hall, "Know you not that I have power to crucify you, and have power to release you?" Jesus was able to reply, "You could have no power at all against me, except it were given you from above" (John 19:10,11). But all that is past, and now the man Christ Jesus is exalted to the Father's right hand, where He awaits the time of His coming again. And when, at length, He comes "Kings shall see and arise, and princes also shall worship" (v.7).

The beauty of the Saviour will dazzle every eye,
In the crowning day that's coming bye and bye.

Three People Groups

But Isaiah brings to our notice an additional, and still future, way in which this Servant will glorify God. It is defined as bringing '*Jacob again to Him,*' '*raising up the tribes of Jacob; and restoring the preserved of Israel*' (v.5,6). Following His initial rejection by Israel, the song discloses that the Servant's mission will be renewed and expanded and, eventually, it will be brought to a successful completion. And the chosen nation, now restored to the Lord, will become the vehicle of God's blessing to the nations. And in this way, the whole earth will be brought to minister to the glory of God's name.

To appreciate these things, it is necessary both to understand, and to distinguish, the different people groups that are before us in the scriptures. Three such groups were plainly identified by Paul: (i) *the Jews*, (ii) *the Gentiles*, and (iii) *the Church of God*. (See 1Cor.10:32.) And since God is always working towards His own glory, it is certain that the glory of God will be manifested in connection with each of these groups.

Gentiles and Jews

The Bible begins with the record of creation and the subsequent fall of the entire human race in Adam. At the beginning of the human story, the universal headship of Adam meant that all had their origin in him. And through Adam's headship all were involved in the fall. Whether we accept it or not, the Bible teaching on this point is indisputable. The suffering under which the whole creation groans today is not the result of design, but of a tremendous catastrophe which brought ruin and misery in its train.

Later, there followed the judgement of the great flood. And then, after some time, God called Abraham from his idolatry in Mesopotamia, and promised to make of him a great nation. Abraham's seed in due course became the nation of Israel, which, in turn, became the pivotal point around which it was intended that the government of the whole earth would be established. This meant that from the call of Abraham forward there were two separate peoples upon the earth, (i) *the nation of Israel* and (ii) *the Gentile nations*. Paul drew a sharp distinction between them when he wrote of the latter, they were "aliens from the commonwealth of Israel, and strangers from the covenants of promise" (Eph.2:12).

Individual Salvation

While recognising this to be true, we do not overlook the fact that many individual Gentiles were saved during the Old Testament period. We need only think of Rahab and of Ruth, both of whom feature in the genealogy of Jesus. Then there was Naaman, the leper from Syria, who was cleansed of his leprosy in the days of the prophet Elisha. He was probably one the most notable person to be saved from among the Gentiles during that time.

But there were many others besides. In the house of Cornelius, Peter declared "that God is no respecter of persons; but in every nation he that fears Him, and works righteousness, is accepted with Him" (Acts 10:34,35). Yet all who were saved in that period had one thing in common. While they did not become Jews in an ethnic sense, they did come to recognise Israel's God as the one true and living God.

By the same token, during that period many persons of faith were found in Israel. Hebrews chapter eleven gives a long, but not exhaustive, list of men and women of faith. But the interesting thing is that no one was automatically considered a person of faith, simply because they had been born within the chosen nation. This highlights a matter of great importance. It teaches us that there is nothing mechanical or automatic, about true spiritual experience, either in their day or in ours.

Before an individual could take his place as a true Israelite, that person had to present the atonement money, the half shekel of silver, according to the shekel of the sanctuary. This was a quite specific legal requirement. "The rich shall not give more, and the poor shall not give less ... to make an atonement for your souls" (Ex.30:15). In this way it was established that, even in the case of persons who had all the privileges Gentiles did not enjoy, salvation was still an individual matter.

"For he is not a Jew who is one outwardly: neither is that circumcision which is outward in the flesh; but He is a Jew who is one inwardly: and circumcision is that of the heart, in the spirit and not in the letter; whose praise is not of men, but of God" (Rom.2:28,29). When it comes to religious profession, this principle is just as true for us. Outward circumstance may suggest one thing while the inward reality may be quite different.

The Church

Over against the Jew and the Gentile, the New Testament introduces a third group known as *the Church*. This group is different from the others both (i) as to its place in history, for it is unique to this present inter-advent period; and (ii) as to its composition, for it is made up only of saved individuals, who are called from among both the Jews and the Gentiles.

The Mystery

The New Testament speaks of the church as a mystery, which in other ages was not made known unto the sons of men. (See Eph.3:5.) This has sometimes puzzled readers of scripture, for in the Old Testament we do have a clear and definite purpose of God for the Gentile nations. They are one day to be given to Messiah as an inheritance. (See Psa.2:8.) And the original promise to Abraham pledged that all the nations of the earth would be blessed through his seed. (See Gen.12:3.) But the precise thing that had not been made known was that the unique position of Israel, as the chosen people of God, would be temporarily interrupted, and replaced by a new international community known as the Church.

The Church, the mystical body of Christ, was formed at Pentecost by the baptism of the Spirit. And now, at conversion, all who repent and believe the gospel are made partakers of that baptism, and in this way they are incorporated in the Church. (See 1Cor.12:13.) Since all such are members together in the body of Christ, it follows that they are members one of another.

Organically united to Christ, believing Jews and Gentiles together, and without distinction, now form the Church. Paul wrote of this new arrangement "There is neither Jew nor Greek ... for you are all one in Christ Jesus" (Gal.3:28). This special bond or relationship overrides every earthly distinction, whether racial or national. Whatever differences there may be among them, this is the common bond that makes them one.

The Heavenly Calling

In contrast to national Israel whose sphere is on the earth, the Church's home is in heaven. Called with a heavenly calling, the Church presses towards a heavenly hope. Her blessings are said to be, in Christ, in heavenly places. "Blessed be the God and Father of our Lord Jesus Christ, who has blessed us with all spiritual blessings in heavenly places in Christ" (Eph.1:3). In the purpose of God the Church is also destined to become Christ's bride.

The Church is spoken of as a mystery that was hidden from past ages, and is not, therefore, the subject of Old Testament prophecy. But when the time came for the mystery to be made known, it was revealed very largely through the ministry of the apostle Paul. Because of this, it is to the epistles of the New Testament, and especially to the epistles of Paul, we must turn to learn the truth of the Church. (See Eph.3:1-6 and Col.1:25-27.)

Some would belittle the ministry of Paul. Their cry is 'Back to Jesus' as though there were discrepancies between Paul and Jesus. But the disciples had already been instructed that the Holy Spirit would show them *things to come*. (See John 16:12-15.) These things, which were consequent upon the setting aside of Israel, were made known by the Spirit through human instruments. Short of the ascended Lord Jesus coming back in person, there was no other way for this to be done, but by human instruments. Among those instruments, Paul's oral and written ministries must be accorded a chief place.

Gospel Preaching

After His resurrection, the risen Lord commissioned the disciples to preach the gospel to every creature, and that remains our task to this day. By the gospel we mean the good news of a Saviour who is able to save men and women from both the guilt and power of sin. "This is a faithful saying, and worthy of all acceptance, that Christ Jesus came into the world to save sinners" (1Tim.1:15). The saving of sinners involved His dying, for it was by His death He made atonement for sin. And it is on the basis of that atonement, the risen Lord Jesus waits to receive all who will come to Him in repentance and in faith.

For the purposes of evangelism no difference is recognised today between Jew and Gentile. "There is no difference between the Jew and the Greek; for the same Lord over all is rich unto all that call upon Him. For whosoever shall call upon the name of the Lord shall be saved" (Rom.10:12,13). That the great multitude of Gentiles would reject the gospel is clearly anticipated, and yet large numbers have received the good news and embraced the Saviour on the basis of individual trust.

But the gospel was never intended to be an end in itself; it is rather a means to an end. For this reason, while all who believe the gospel are saved, none are saved in isolation. Upon believing, the saved are joined to the Lord as members of His body. This means that the ultimate goal of gospel preaching looks beyond the conversion of individual sinners, to the building up of the Church, the body of Christ. A great weakness of much earnest evangelism is that individual conversion is seen as the end in view, rather than the building up of the church which is God's plain purpose in this age.

Missionary Endeavour

And this is the proper goal of missionary endeavour as well. The salvation of the whole world is not our aim. On the contrary, scripture teaches us that God has already determined a day when the world will be judged. (See Acts17:31.) But the evangelisation of the world is a quite different matter. While judgement tarries, the gospel of individual salvation is to be preached to all, as the divinely appointed means of calling out a separate people to become the spiritual stones that make up God's spiritual house.

This great enterprise will not fail for Jesus said, "I will build my church, and the gates of hell shall not prevail against it" (Matt.16:18). Here is the plainest statement of the present divine intention. Let all who engage in evangelistic ministry, either at home or on the various mission fields of the world, keep this heavenly blueprint before them. In doing so they will preserve themselves from much that might otherwise discourage them.

The Strategic Goal (Cont.)

I will be glorified (ii)

All these amazing projects involving the three people groups (the Jew, the Gentile and the Church), how they will be accomplished, and how they will minister to the glory of God, present us with a study that is at once challenging and rewarding. It was clearly established by the prophets in the Old Testament scriptures, that national Israel will be brought again to the Lord and, then, using Israel as a channel of His peace, the Lord will reach out in blessing to the nations.

The Mystery Revealed

But what some have failed to apprehend is that the mystery, the Church, was not made known in the Old Testament. Of course, with all the light of the New Testament available to us we are able now to look back and see in those earlier scriptures, types, pictures, and shadows of the future Church. But *the Church which is His body* is not an Old Testament concept. The Church's calling, her standing and her destiny, are revealed only in the New Testament.

Nor could it have been otherwise, since it is only as the risen and glorified man that Christ is spoken of as the Head of the Church. "And He is the head of the body, the church; who is the beginning, the firstborn from the dead" (Col.1:18). It follows, therefore, that the Church could have had no existence on earth, until after the Head had taken His proper place in glory.

Writing to the Colossians, Paul described himself as "a minister according to the dispensation of God which is given to me for you, to fulfil the word of God, *Even the mystery which has been hidden from ages and from generations, but now is made manifest* to His saints" (Col.1:25,26). In similar vein he wrote to the Ephesians of his "knowledge in the mystery of Christ. *Which in other ages was not made known to the sons of men, as it is now revealed* to His holy apostles and prophets by the Spirit: That the Gentiles should be fellow heirs, and of the same body, and partakers of His promise in Christ by the gospel" (Eph.3:4-6).

These scriptures clearly imply that the present Church age is unique among all the ages and dispensations of God's dealings with men. The present age is perhaps best thought of simply as an interval between the setting aside of national Israel, on the one hand, and Israel's restoration on the other. The Church age, therefore, should be viewed as a transitional period, an interruption in the outworking of God's purposes respecting Israel and the nations.

The End of the Age

We have noted already how this Church age began, but how it will end is also the subject of special revelation. Paul wrote to the church at Corinth, "Behold I show you a mystery: we shall not all sleep, but we shall all be changed, in a moment, in the twinkling of an eye, at the last trump ... " (1Cor.15:51,52). In another letter the apostle amplified this statement. Anticipating that momentous moment, and the sounding of the trump of God, he wrote, "The dead in Christ shall rise first; then we who are alive and remain shall be caught up together with them in the clouds, to meet the Lord in the air; and so shall we ever be with the Lord" (1Thess.4:16,17).

At the coming of the Lord to the air, a resurrection will take place which will be like Christ's own resurrection. It will be not just a resurrection *of the dead*, but a resurrection *out from among the dead*. Certain ones, the dead in Christ, will rise, while the rest of the dead will remain unaffected by what has happened, for at least a thousand years. This is the first resurrection. The scripture also says, "Blessed and holy is he who has part in the first resurrection" (Rev.20:6). The notion of a general resurrection of the dead, embracing those who are in Christ and those who are not, falls far short of what is here revealed through Paul.

The Christian Hope

All these references clearly envision the promised return of our Lord Jesus Christ. They proclaim the resurrection of believers, and they point to what is often referred to as the rapture of the Church. The pledge given by the Lord Jesus on the eve of His dying encompasses all these things. He said, "I will come again, and receive you unto myself" (John14.3). This glorious prospect constitutes the Church's proper hope. And this calling away of the Church is also the specific event that will mark the close of the present age.

The Coming in two parts

Another factor of great importance is that the Lord's return itself will be in two stages: He will come first *to the air* and then *to the earth.* In a most significant passage, after identifying the first stage in the Lord's return, Paul went on to deal with the second stage. He even listed some of the events that will take place during the period between the two stages. Notable among them will be the appearing of the Antichrist and the time of great tribulation that will come upon the earth.

The passage we refer to says, "Now we beseech you, brethren, by *the coming of our Lord Jesus Christ, and by our gathering together unto Him ...* " This seems to refer to the rapture of the Church, at the coming to the air. And then moving on to the second stage, the coming to the earth, he writes, "*And then shall that wicked one be revealed, whom the Lord shall consume with the spirit of His mouth, and shall destroy with the brightness of His coming*" (2Thess.2:1-8). The apostolic argument seems quite clear. He outlines the order of events; before antichrist can be judged he must be revealed, and before he can be revealed the Church must be removed. Therefore, before the Lord Jesus returns to the earth to establish the messianic kingdom, He will come to the air to receive the Church to Himself.

Simply by way of illustration of these things, we might think of Enoch and of Noah in the days before the flood. Before the coming of the great flood through which Noah passed, Enoch was translated; so in a similar way, before the great tribulation comes through which Israel and the nations will pass, the Church will be caught up to meet the Lord in the air. Only then, and after an interval of time, will the Lord come to the earth to execute judgement, and to establish the messianic kingdom. This is Israel's hope. And as such, it is the surpassing theme of Old Testament prophecy in general, and of Isaiah's servant songs in particular.

The Early Church in Committee

Several contentious issues having arisen in the early church, a great council was called in Jerusalem, to discuss them. (See Acts 15:13-18.) At its conclusion, the apostle James, who seems to have been in the chair, gave his judgement. He said, "Simeon [Peter] has declared how God first did visit the Gentiles, to take out of them a people for His name." Here we have God's present purpose, the calling out of the Church through the preaching of the gospel.

The Tabernacle of David

James then added, "To this agree the words of the prophets, as it is written: *After this* I will return and will build again the tabernacle of David, which is fallen down; and I will build again its ruins, and I will set it up." This prediction quite plainly refers to the theocratic kingdom of David and Solomon which will be re-established in the earth at the time of the Lord's return.

The extended prophecy goes on, "In that day will I raise up the tabernacle of David that is fallen, and close up the breaches of it; and I will raise up his ruins, and I will build it as in the days of old ... And I will plant them upon their land, and they shall no more be pulled out of their land which I have given them, saith the Lord, thy God." (See Amos 9:11-15.) Patently the day for these things is not yet, but that it will come is beyond doubt.

And so, while not the subject of Old Testament prophecy, there is nothing inconsistent about the Church being God's purpose in this present age. This age of the Church is, as we have already indicated, simply an interval in God's dealings with the seed of Abraham. Remarkably, the interval itself, although not what would occupy it, was envisaged in several Old Testament passages.

One of the millennial psalms begins like this, "The Lord said unto my Lord, Sit thou at my right hand, *until* I make thine enemies thy footstool" (Psa.110:1). The first part of the verse is already fulfilled. For the risen Lord Jesus said, "I am set down with my Father in His throne" (Rev.3:21). The second part awaits a future day for its fulfilment, and we are now living in the interval that lies between.

Discipling the Nations

But James had a third thing to say at the conclusion of the Jerusalem council, he went on to speak of God's plan for the nations after Israel has been restored. "That the residue of men might seek after the Lord, and all the nations, upon whom my name is called, saith the Lord, who doeth all these things." Here we have the divine intention for the Gentile nations, the last of our three people groups. James clearly recognised that the blessing of the nations will be dependent on the prior blessing of Israel.

However much it may offend our rather parochial way of looking at things, it is beyond doubt that the Lord has other astonishing objectives, besides the conversion of individual sinners, and the calling out of the Church. He will yet send forth His angels with a great sound of a trumpet, to gather together His elect from the four winds, from one end of heaven to the other. (See Matt.24:31.) And after that, all flesh shall see the glory of the Lord, for His glory will be revealed in a manner without parallel in the long tale of human history.

And in the end, the living God will have His way, for nothing can thwart His purpose or resist His will. He is able to make the wrath of man to praise Him, and after that to still its fury. The specific word spoken by Isaiah in this second song must also have its answer. The Servant-King, who was despised by men and abhorred by the nation, will be so startlingly revealed that "*kings shall see and arise, and princes also shall worship*" (Isa.49:7).

Egypt's Pharaoh might decry, "Who is the Lord, that I should obey His voice to let Israel go?" (Ex.5:2) And the haughty Nebuchadnezzar might proudly boast, "Is not this great Babylon, that I have built ... by the might of my power, and for the honour of my majesty?" (Dan.4:30) But in the end, both must humbly bow down and acknowledge Him, "Who has prepared His throne in the heavens, and whose kingdom rules over all" (Psa. 103:19).

A Present Application

Of course, we must carefully distinguish between this promised blessing of the nations which is still future, and the universal proclamation of the gospel today. In that day, God's purpose will be the restoration of national Israel, and the eventual blessing of the nations in the kingdom period. The purpose of God in the present age, however, is to call out the Church, by the preaching of the gospel. A failure to recognise this revealed order, and to discern the distinction between the Church of today, and the kingdom of that future day, has been the cause of much needless confusion.

With the realisation of these things, an astonishing prediction found in another of the great millennial psalms will also have its fulfillment, "He shall have dominion from sea to sea, and from the river to the ends of the earth. All nations shall call Him blessed, and the whole earth shall be filled with His glory" (Psa.72:8,17,19). *James Montgomery* captured this in a well loved hymn-,

Hail to the Lord's anointed, great David's greater Son.
Hail in the time appointed, His reign on earth begun!
He comes to break oppression, to set the captive free:
To take away transgression, and rule in equity.

Kings shall fall down before Him,
and gold and incense bring;
All nations shall adore Him, His praise all people sing:
For He shall have dominion o'er river, sea, and shore,
Far as the eagle's pinion or dove's light wing can soar.

2. The Tactical Plan

To Bring Jacob again (v.5)

The grand theme that runs through the entire Old Testament, giving unity to the whole, is the person of our redeeming Lord. The Lord Jesus once described the Hebrew Scriptures in these words, "These are they which testify of me." He emphasised the same thing on another occasion, when He gave what must have been a masterful exposition of those same scriptures. "Beginning at Moses, and all the prophets, He expounded unto them, in all the scriptures, the things concerning Himself" (Luke 24:27).

This theme, like a golden thread, also links the two testaments, the old and the new. Our wonderful Bible is like the silver trumpets which Moses commanded were to be beaten out of one piece of silver, there were two trumpets, yet just one instrument. (See Numbers 10.) In the same way we have two Testaments, but just one Bible.

It has been rightly pointed out on many occasions that the Gospels belong as much to the Old Testament as to the New, since the four Evangelists combine to record the ministry of Jesus as the Jews' long awaited Messiah. The opening verse of the New Testament speaks of Him as "the son of David, the son of Abraham" (Matt.1:1).

The Purposes behind the Incarnation

With this in mind we might call attention again to the fact that there were two distinct dimensions to the incarnation. The first was *mediatorial*, "Christ Jesus came into the world to save sinners" (1Tim.1:15). Since this is what most immediately impacts us, we have a tendency to dwell almost exclusively on this side of the incarnation. The other is the *messianic* dimension and this is what is mainly highlighted in these songs. This side of things is essentially national in character, and while it has definite and far reaching implications for every man, its primary object is the nation of Israel.

The incarnate Christ is presented first of all, as 'the King of the Jews' (Matt.2:1,2). And He repeatedly stressed this aspect of His mission. On one occasion He said, "I am not sent but to the lost sheep of the house of Israel" (Matt.15:24). And when sending forth the twelve to preach, He instructed them, "Go not into the way of the Gentiles, and into any city of the Samaritans enter not; but go, rather, to the lost sheep of the house of Israel" (Matt.10:5,6).

When He rode into Jerusalem on a borrowed colt, just a few days before the crucifixion, the prophecy of Zechariah was fulfilled which said, "Rejoice greatly, O daughter of Zion; shout, O daughter of Jerusalem; behold, your King comes unto you; He is just, and having salvation; lowly, and riding upon an ass, and upon a colt, the foal of an ass" (Zech.9:9). And it must be significant that when on the cross, the writing placed above His head, and written in three languages read, "This is Jesus, the King of the Jews" (Matt.27:37).

The Seed of David

Such references can only be properly understood in the light of the Davidic covenant. And that covenant is certainly the background against which we should read the Servant Songs. (See 2Sam.7:12-17.) David had resolved to build a temple to the Lord, and the prophet Nathan encouraged him to proceed, and do all that was in his heart. But it was not God's will that David should do this thing, and Nathan had to go back and correct his earlier advice. David's son would build the temple for he would be a man of peace, whereas David himself had been a man of war.

But the temple concept was sound in principle, and God honoured David for it. He did so by making a covenant with him in which He said, "Thy house and thy kingdom shall be established for ever before thee; thy throne shall be established forever" (2Sam.7:16). That these things are not to be understood in some spiritual or non-literal sense is evident from the fact that it was Solomon, David's immediate successor, who actually built the magnificent temple at Jerusalem.

In the covenant the Lord promised to David a seed, in perpetuity, one who would sit upon his throne. The promise clearly looked beyond David's immediate successors in Jerusalem, to the Lord Jesus Christ. And so when Jesus was born of Mary, it was emphasised that He was born of David's line, and that all the pledges of the Davidic covenant were vested in Him. The carefully detailed genealogies in the first and third gospels show, beyond all doubt, that His descent could be traced back to David, and to Abraham, and even to Adam. Quite plainly the entitlement of Mary's firstborn to the Davidic dynasty was well founded.

Hence the angel Gabriel's announcement to the virgin mother concerning the child soon to be born: "the Lord God shall give unto Him the throne of His father David. And He shall reign over the house of Jacob forever; and of His kingdom there shall be no end" (Luke1:32,33). Mary could have understood Gabriel's words in only one way; they could mean just one thing. The long awaited kingdom was about to come. The messianic promises given centuries before, to Abraham and to David, were about to be realised.

Messianic Promises

It is equally clear that this messianic dimension to the incarnation formed a major part in the predictions of the Hebrew Seers. And when Isaiah's Servant speaks in this second song and says, "And now, saith the Lord, who formed me from the womb to be His servant, *to bring Jacob again to Him ...* " (v.5), it is this same messianic dimension that is indicated.

Many years after Isaiah had died, the people of Judah were languishing in captivity in the land of Babylon. It was then that political authority came into the hands of Cyrus, the Persian. And in the unerring providence of God, Cyrus, was moved to sign an historic decree which allowed the exiled people to return home to Zion. The return, when it took place, was in three stages. These were led respectively by Zerubbabel, Ezra and Nehemiah. Those who came back rebuilt the Temple and the city walls of Jerusalem. It was a mighty enterprise, full of promise and, on the whole, it was carried through with great enthusiasm.

An essential factor in that return from Babylon was that the chosen people should be in the land to receive their Messiah at His first coming. For the moment, we will pass over the treatment He received at the hands of the people to whom He came. But we must note that the circumstances of His birth, the manner of His ministry, and the miracles He wrought, were all in complete accord with the messianic prophecies that had gone before. In addition, His presentation to Israel was said to have been in the fullness of time.

Unfulfilled Prophecy

And yet while all this is true, it still has to be conceded that a whole raft of prophecies remained that just could not have been fulfilled in the return from Babylon. We refer to prophecies that look beyond that first recovery to a greater and more significant recovery in the last days. Prophecies that anticipate the chosen people's final establishment in their own land. The multitude of such prophecies are too numerous for us to catalogue in these pages. We shall select just a few.

Moses

Going back as far as Moses we find that a dispersion, greater than the captivity in Babylon, was foreseen even in those days. "And it shall come to pass, when all these things are come upon you, the blessing and the curse, which I have set before you, and you shall call them to mind *among all the nations*, to which the Lord your God has driven you, and shall return unto the Lord your God ... that then the Lord your God will turn your captivity, and have compassion upon you, and will return and gather you *from all the nations* where the Lord your God has scattered you" (Deut.30:1-3).

Ezekiel

The prophet Ezekiel, who ministered during the period of the exile in Babylon, spoke in similar vein. Before proclaiming the future cleansing and regeneration of the remnant of Israel, he said, "I will take you *from among the nations*, and gather you *out of all countries*, and will bring you into your own land." Such pledges presuppose that the people are exiled from their own land, not just to a single country like Babylon, but that they are scattered among all countries.

In the same context Ezekiel declared, "The nations shall know that I am the Lord, when I shall be sanctified in you before their eyes." (See Ezk.36:23,24.) These references to a future regathering of the dispersed of Israel from all nations is the restoration to the land of promise in the last days which, in turn, will lead on to the blessing of the Gentile nations in the messianic kingdom.

Paul

In a very significant passage Paul used the olive tree as a figure of the purpose of God. He saw the natural branches (Israel) broken off for a time, and then, in the end, grafted in again. This regrafting of Israel is seen to take place in the context of 'the Deliverer coming out of Sion' and of 'all Israel being saved.' (See Romans 11:26.) He then went on to argue that if Israel's temporary setting aside has resulted in the blessing of the gospel coming to the Gentiles, then what will Israel's restoration be, but as life from the dead.

This is also the message of the second servant song. It predicts the blessing of God flowing out to the nations, through the prior renewal and restoration of Israel. The word of God concerning the Servant is this, "It is a light thing that you should be my servant to raise up the tribes of Jacob, and to restore the preserved of Israel; I will also give you for a light to the nations, that you may be my salvation to the ends of the earth" (Isa.49:6).

Behold the mountain of the Lord
In latter days shall rise
On mountain tops above the hills
And draw the wondering eyes.
The beam that shines from Zion's hill
Shall lighten every land;
The King who reigns in Salem's towers
Shall all the world command.

A Broader Application

While stressing these future events, and emphasising the primary interpretation of these scriptures, we do not ignore the fact that the enlarged mission of the Servant does have a certain application to the present time. It was the risen Christ Himself who laid upon His disciples the responsibility of being His witnesses "to the uttermost parts of the earth" (Acts 1:8).

And not long afterwards, when the Jews at Antioch refused the grace of God, proclaimed to them by Paul and Barnabas, the apostles' only course was to turn to the Gentiles. In doing so they justified their action by quoting this part of the second song. (See Acts13:47.)

But we cannot too strongly emphasise that any application of these words to the apostles, or to ourselves, in the course of this age, does not annul the clearly stated purpose of God for national Israel and the Gentile nations in a coming day.

Jeremiah ministered both before and during the Babylonian exile. He, too, predicted a restoration of the nation that can only be still future. He said, "Behold, the days come, saith the Lord, that I will raise unto David a righteous Branch, and a king shall reign and prosper, and shall execute justice and righteousness in the earth. In his days Judah shall be saved, and Israel shall dwell safely; and this is his name whereby he shall be called, The Lord our righteousness" (Jer.23:5,6).

It should be carefully noted that Jeremiah's prediction, is given to the nation as a whole: it is given to all twelve tribes, *Judah shall be saved, and Israel ...* The pledge then is clear, the people will become one nation again, and no longer two, as they have been for so long. All these many predictions, while they obviously look beyond the return of the exiles from Babylon, look even beyond this present period of time to a still future and final gathering together of Israel in the last days.

The *Second Song*

3. The Present Stalemate

Though Israel be not gathered (v.5)

From the beginning of His incarnate state, it is clear that the Lord Jesus had the kingdom goal before His mind. The first instruction of His public ministry was to teach His disciples to pray for the establishment of a kingdom in which God's will would be done in earth as it is in heaven. This kingdom, for which we still pray, will require for its institution the bringing of '*Jacob again to the Lord,*' and the *'raising up the tribes of Jacob, and the restoring the preserved of Israel'* (v.5,6).

In every generation, prophets had been raised up to bear witness to the very things that are spoken of in these songs, and to the one whom God would send. Yet, when the time came and Messiah presented Himself, the leaders of the people were unable to find a good word to say about Him. When He cast out demons, they said He did this by Beelzebub, the prince of demons. As His earthly ministry drew to a close, besides being rejected, He was actually despised by the very people He had come to serve.

It is now a matter of history that in spite of all the advantages with which they had been so richly endowed, Israel would have none of Him. They were the chosen people, to them had been committed the oracles of God and the commandments. Such privileges should have humbled them, but they had become proud of their status as the people of God, and when Messiah came they saw no beauty in Him, that they should desire Him. They smote the Judge of Israel with a rod upon the cheek. And, in the end, nothing would satisfy them short of His crucifixion.

God's Longsuffering

Although Israel's rejection of her Messiah would lead to the suspension, for a time, of the kingdom promises, nevertheless, the Lord was loath to forsake His people, whom He had chosen. Just as, in Ezekiel's vision (See Ezk. 10.), the glory cloud was loath to leave the temple and the city, so the Lord, even in the aftermath of His rejection, still yearned after His people Israel.

The proof of this was demonstrated, in a very telling way, on the occasion of the healing of the lame man at the beautiful gate of the Temple. The healing became the backdrop for Peter's second pentecostal sermon. The first sermon gathered around the events of the first advent, but the second centred on the second advent. (See Acts3:1-26.)

The incredulous multitude heard Peter fearlessly press home their great sin in denying the Holy One, and desiring a murderer in His stead. But even this great sin, the preacher put down to the ignorance that was in them by nature. In this way, Peter brought their great sin within the range of God's pardoning grace, because there was no forgiveness for wilful sin. He then followed this with an astonishing pronouncement. It was to the effect that, if they would yet repent and humble themselves, even at so late a stage, God would blot out their sins and actually send the Lord Jesus who had so recently risen from the dead and ascended to heaven. (See Acts 3:19,20.)

It was an extraordinary declaration. If Israel would even now turn to the Lord in true repentance, God would send Jesus, and those millennial conditions would be realised which had been spoken of by all the prophets since the world began. The profoundly significant healing of the lame man, therefore, was the occasion of a further offer of the kingdom to Israel. Here was a striking instance of the longsuffering of God.

What might have been

Outwardly, the nation at that time was represented by the Temple with its regular services, all of which were maintained with commendable zeal. But inwardly, the nation was like the lame man, spiritually impotent, and unable to walk and to please God. It took a miracle to transform the lame man. Nothing less would have enabled him to stand up and walk, and to enter the Temple with the apostles, walking and leaping and praising God.

This most notable miracle, therefore, is an illustration in two parts: in the first place it pictures what would have been had the nation received her Messiah. But He had been rejected. And now to this further offer, the nation was soon to give its answer in the martyrdom of Stephen. So the miracle, in the second place, serves to illustrate what shall be when the Saviour comes again.

Only then will Israel, in repentance and faith, look upon Him whom they pierced. (See Zech.12:10.) That look of faith will give rise to a miracle of national regeneration, and the nation (or at least a remnant of it) will be transformed to become like the lame man, now healed, at the beautiful gate. When that happens, it will be a dramatic fulfilment of the prophecy which says, "The lame man shall leap as an hart, and the tongue of the dumb shall sing" (Isa.35:6).

The question is often asked, "What would have happened if the nation had received her king?" The healing of the lame man is the short answer. But the nearest the Lord Himself came to answering that inquiry directly was when He wept over Jerusalem and said, "If you had known ... the things which belong to your peace! But now they are hidden from your eyes" (Luke 19:42). With these words He drew a veil over what might have been, and we cannot speak where He is silent.

The Kingdom Adjourned

The treatment meted out to the Lord Jesus when He came as the messenger of the covenant, is already well documented. What is not always recognised, however, is that the rejection of Christ, the King, resulted in the postponement of the promised messianic kingdom, and the initiation of a wholly new enterprise known as the Church. Having already emphasised this, we stress it again for it is necessary to an understanding of these things.

In the purposes of God the chosen people have been set aside, they have been quite literally scattered among all nations. They are now experiencing a second, long drawn out, dispersion. But while this continues to be Israel's condition to the present day, it is not the end of the story. For God has ordained that in the last days Israel will be physically regathered to the land of promise and spiritually restored to the Lord their God.

Postponed for a time

"Your house is left unto you desolate" was Messiah's heartfelt lament over an unresponsive people on that memorable occasion when He wept over their city. Can anyone doubt that this has been a fair description of Israel's condition for almost two thousand years? But Israel's desolation is not forever. The Lord Jesus envisaged a day when the penitent nation will say, "Blessed is He that comes in the name of the Lord" (Matt.23:37-39).

On another occasion He warned the Jews of the trials that would befall their city, trials which came to pass when the Roman army, under Titus, sacked Jerusalem in AD70. He forewarned His hearers, "*They shall fall by the edge of the sword.*" He even went on to predict, "*They shall be led away captive into all nations.*" And He further declared, "*Jerusalem shall be trodden down by the Gentiles*." All these forebodings have been factually fulfilled over the centuries. Yet this state of affairs will not last forever, although it will continue "*until the Times of the Gentiles*" are fulfilled, (See Luke 21:24.)

Paul too, referred to the judicial, albeit partial, blindness that is upon Israel today. "Even to this day, when Moses is read, the veil is upon their heart." But neither is this a permanent affliction for he went on to say, "Nevertheless, when it [*i.e.* the nation] shall turn to the Lord, *the veil shall be taken away*" (2Cor.3:15,16). Desolate, trodden down and judically blinded. What a perceptive description of Israel's lot across the centuries of this present era.

Israel's Partial Blindness

But the blindness that is now upon Israel is not final, and we must stress that is it not total. Discussing Israel's present dispersion and future recovery, Paul called attention to a most marvelleous thing. There is even now, "*a remnant according to the election of grace*" (Rom.11:5). Through the years there have always been individual Jews, who have turned to the Lord, and confessed Jesus as their Messiah and Saviour. Just as it was among the Gentiles in the old dispensation, many were saved, so it is among the Jews today. Moreover, the believing Jews of this present age, are viewed as an earnest of the future ingathering of the nation.

A parallel to this can be seen in the period of Israel's wilderness wanderings. The plainly stated purpose of God at that time was to bring His people out of Egypt, across the desert, and into the land of Canaan. When they came to Kadesh Barnea the first two parts of the divine plan had effectively been accomplished. But because of their unbelief at Kadesh the third part was postponed for a generation. During the intervening years Caleb and Joshua constituted a very small, but very significant, minority. In view of the promises given to them, they actually embodied in a living way Israel's hope of entry into the land.

A Remnant Remains

Similarly, in this present interval of the church, while national Israel has been set aside, there always have been Jews who have believed the gospel. Together with believing Gentiles, they share equally the privilege of being part of the body of Christ. But more than that, their very existence, like a beacon, keeps alive the messianic hope: the hope that Israel, now dispersed, will finally be restored to the Lord. They do this in much the same way as Caleb and Joshua kept alive the hope of entry into the land, during the thirty eight years of wandering in the wilderness.

The day is surely coming when Israel's hope of national and spiritual revival will be realised. And when it takes place, the recovery will parallel her original redemption from Egypt. The second stanza of our song carries us forward to that glorious time, when millennial conditions shall be introduced throughout the earth. Then the Servant's mission will at last be accomplished, His vision will be realised. In the meantime, we seem to hear Him say, "*Though Israel be not gathered, yet shall I be glorious in the eyes of the Lord ...* " (Isa.49:5).

Then shall Israel long dispersed,
Mourning, seek the Lord their God.
Look on Him whom once they pierced,
Own and kiss the chastening rod.
Then all Israel shall be saved,
War and tumult then shall cease,
While the greater Son of David,
Rules a conquered world in peace.

4. The Ultimate Trimuph

A Light to the Nations (v.6)

As He passed through this world the Lord Jesus "Offered up prayers and supplications with strong crying and tears unto Him that was able to save Him from death, and was heard in that He feared" (Hebs.5:7). The second song gives us an insight into how those prayers were answered, "*Thus says the Lord: In an acceptable time have I heard you, and in a day of salvation have I helped you ...* " (v.8).

His bodily resurrection on the third day was the immediate answer to those prayers; God vindicated Him by raising Him from the dead. An even more complete answer, however, looks beyond the resurrection to His return when God will again vindicate His Son. But this time He will do so in a very public manner. "*In an acceptable time have I heard you, and in a day of salvation have I helped you; I will preserve you, and give you for a covenant of the people, to restore the land, and to reassign its desolate inheritances*" (v.8 *n.i.v.*). All these pledges will be redeemed when the Davidic kingdom is restored, and David's people are brought again to enjoy their promised inheritance.

Isaiah repeatedly applied the language of 'the desolate places' to the land of Israel. (See Isa.1:7,6:11,17:9 etc.) Here he insists that *the land and the desolate places will be inhabited* (v.8). Later he amplified this assertion, saying "And they shall build the old wastes, they shall raise up the former desolations, and they shall repair the waste cities, the desolations of many generations" (Isa.61:4). There is a wonderful consistency about these visions of the future kingdom and of Israel's ascendency in it.

But the prophet went on to say that *liberty will also be proclaimed to the captives and obscurity will give way to a clear shining* (v.9). Some see the fulfilment of this in the return of the exiles from Babylon, but like so many of the prophetic scriptures it probably has both a near and a distant fulfilment. While it may take account of the return of the captives, and doubtless they found strength for their journey in Isaiah's words, the prophecy evidently looked beyond them to the ultimate gathering together of the outcasts of Israel and the dispersed of Judah, in the day of Messiah's reign.

The Shepherd and his Sheep

The imagery of the shepherd and his sheep is common enough in scripture. Here the perfect Servant is viewed as the Shepherd of Israel in millennial times. "*They will feed beside the roads and find pasture on every barren hill. They will neither hunger nor thirst, nor will the desert heat or the sun beat upon them. He who has compassion on them will guide them and lead them beside springs of water*" (v. 9,10 *n.i.v.*). Their confidence in that day may very well find its expression, as ours so often does to-day, in the familiar words of the twenty third psalm, "The Lord is my shepherd, I shall not want."

At the time of His first advent the Lord Jesus came as the good shepherd to give His life for the sheep, and now, in resurrection, He is the great shepherd of His people. But our song has in view His second advent, when He shall tend restored Israel with all the care of a loving shepherd for a needy flock. He will bring His scattered sheep from great distances and from all points of the compass, even some from as far away as the region of Sinim (v.12), which many scholars identify with China.

However obscure some of these things may be to us, we can be sure they will become abundantly clear as the hour approaches. This much is beyond question: nothing will hinder the working out of God's purposes concerning His chosen people, for "the gifts and calling of God are without repentance" (Rom.11:29). When the Lord stretches out His hand again to recover the remnant of His people, every obstacle in the way of their return will be removed.

Israel in the Twentieth Century

Of the many remarkable developments that took place in the twentieth century, none is more significant, from the standpoint of Bible prophecy, than the resurgence of Israel to become a nation once again. Israel is not the oldest of the nations, but no other nation has been deprived of its homeland for so long, and has not only survived, but has also retained its national identity. Who can question that the preserving hand of God has been upon this people during the long drawn out period of their second dispersion.

Moreover, during this long and fateful exile, as we have already noted, a godly remnant has been raised up to keep alive the hope of the glorious future repeatedly predicted by the prophets. How else can we understand what Isaiah said about the watchmen? "I have set watchmen upon thy walls, O Jerusalem, who shall never hold their peace day nor night; you that make mention of the Lord, keep not silence, and give Him no rest, till He establish, and till He make Jerusalem a praise in the earth" (Isa.62:6,7).

"Look down from heaven, and behold from the habitation of thy holiness and of thy glory, Where are thy zeal and thy strength, the yearnings of thine heart and of thy mercies toward me? Are they restrained?" (Isa.63:15) And again this remnant was surely before Isaiah's mind when he wrote, "For Zion's sake will I not hold my peace, and for Jerusalem's sake I will not rest, until her righteousness go forth as brightness, and her salvation as a lamp that burneth ... Thou shalt no more be termed Forsaken, neither shall thy land any more be termed Desolate" (Isa.62:1-4). An echo of these intercessions can also be heard in many of the Psalms as well as in the Prophets.

Theodore Herzl.

When the Jews began to emerge from the ghettoes of Eastern Europe, at the end of the '*Haskalah*' (the period of the Jewish enlightenment) in the 1880s, some of them dared to hope for a land of their own. And around that time the World Zionist Organisation was founded. Its founder, who gave it great impetus, was an Austrian Jew, called Theodore Herzl. In Vienna, in 1884, Herzl gained a doctorate in law, but afterwards he abandoned the legal profession in favour of writing, and very soon became a prolific author.

The idea of a Jewish homeland was not new, but Herzl formulated a definite plan for the re-establishing of a state of Israel, and for the resettlement of the Jewish people in a land of their own. He condensed his arguments in favour of these ideals, and his programme for their accomplishment, into a pamphlet he called, *'Der Judenstaat'* meaning, *'The Jewish state.'* This made an immediate and powerful impact on Jewish thinking at the time. So much so, Herzl declared at the first Zionist Congress in Vienna in 1897, that the Land of Israel would become a reality within 50 years.

Although he did not live to see it, twenty years later and towards the end of the first world war, Palestine was already denoted to become a national home for the Jews. Then, following the second world war, the repatriation of the Jews to their own land was speeded up and greatly facilitated. In 1948 the Jewish people attained to independent nationhood, and since then the rather tenuous hold they had on the land has been consolidated. As a people they have become a sophisticated modern society, perhaps the foremost society in the Middle East today. It was on August 17th 1949 that a grateful people reburied Herzl's remains on a hillside overlooking Jerusalem. That hill is known today as Mount Herzl.

The Six Days' War

The years from then until now have been tumultuous indeed and make fascinating reading. But it was after the six days' war in 1967, that the divided city of Jerusalem was reunited. At that time some rather over zealous students of prophecy announced that 'the Times of the Gentiles' had now come to an end, and that prophecy was being fulfilled before our eyes. They quoted our Lord's words when He said, "Jerusalem shall be trodden down by the Gentiles, until the times of the Gentiles be fulfilled" (Luke 21:24).

While we do not go along with what we perceive to be their over optimistic assertions, we cannot help being impressed by the course these events have taken. They have been comparative only to developments in continental Europe, where the hitherto warring states and nations have drawn together into an amazing entity, which many see as the ancient Roman Empire at last being revived.

It is an historical fact that at the time of the first advent of Jesus Christ, two components were in place that have been absent during the intervening period: (i) the Jews were in the land, albeit as a vassal state, and (ii) the political power in the earth was the Roman Empire. Have things now come full circle? Are we now in the run up to the fulfilment of those events that will usher in our Lord's second advent? These are imponderable questions.

When trouble raises its head in the Middle East, peace loving people everywhere refrain from using extravagant language when they speak of it. This reticence stems from an innate conviction. We all know, not least the leaders of the major powers, that any instability in that whole region has the potential for Armageddon. Nor can we say more than that the developing world scene has all the appearance of a stage being prepared for those events to take place that scripture associates with the last days.

What we can say, however, is that the present estate of the Jewish people and of the Israeli nation, while it may be a precursor of coming events, is not in itself the regathering to the land or the restoration to the Lord that is predicted in the prophetic writings generally, and in the Servant Songs in particular. Those events still lie in the future.

And so, in one grand sweep, this second servant song embraces the two advents of Christ, and all that lies between them. At the first, He was despised by men and abhorred by the nation, but at His coming again, "All nations shall call Him blessed, and the whole earth shall be filled with His glory" (Psa.72:17,19). Addressed to the nations as a whole, the second song ends with the nations being blessed through the blessing of restored Israel.

The *Second Song*

4. The Ultimate Trimuph (Contd.)

I have laboured in vain (v.4)

The Sorrowful Servant

Before leaving the second song we need to go back to the Servant's first coming. The inspired history records that when the shadow of Calvary was already heavily over His path, Jesus cried out, *"Now is my soul troubled"* (John 12:27). We will not presume to think ourselves capable of comprehending the deep emotion that lay behind these words. But for our profit we might humbly inquire into what it was that so deeply affected our Saviour at that precise moment.

The timing of this statement was the final week before the crucifixion. It followed the riding into Jerusalem on the foal of an ass, as predicted by the prophet Zechariah. (See Zech.9:9.) It coincided, therefore, with His final rejection by the nation. From where He stood this rejection by His own people seemed to signal the failure of His mission. It was not something, therefore, that could be shrugged off lightly, and treated as of no consequence. On the contrary, it moved Him to say, "Now is my soul troubled."

The deep sorrow and the pathos that obviously lay behind His words seems to be echoed in the language of our song. When the Father said, "Thou art my servant, in whom I will be glorified" (v.3), His immediate response was to say, "*I have laboured in vain, I have spent my strength for nothing, and in vain*" (v.4). Significantly, this too was said in the context of an unresponsive nation. (*though Israel be not gathered.* v.5) Such was the profound impact rejection had upon our Saviour. Far from being impervious to the treatment He received, He was deeply troubled by it.

Significantly, the evangelist, recorded the Lord's plaint in the context of the Servant Songs. "But though He had done so many miracles before them, yet they believed not on him; That the saying of Isaiah, the prophet, might be fulfilled, which he spoke, Lord who hath believed our report? And to whom hath the arm of the Lord been revealed? Therefore, they could not believe, because that Isaiah said again, He hath blinded their eyes, and hardened their heart; that they should not see with their eyes, nor understand with their heart, and be converted, and I should heal them. These things said Isaiah, when he saw His glory, and spoke of Him" (John 12:37-41).

Discouraged

Did the Lord Jesus ever suffer discouragement? Was He ever despondent? These are intriguing questions. On one occasion, after spelling out the conditions and the cost of discipleship we are told, "from that time many of His disciples went back, and walked no more with Him." Although "He knew what was in man and needed not that any should testify of man," He was very deeply affected by the defection of so many at that time. We read that He turned to the twelve and said, "Will you also go away?" (See John 2:25; 6:66,67.)

Again, only a week after clamouring to take Him by force and make Him their king, the fickle crowd demanded His death. What must His thoughts have been in these and other similar situations? It is inconceivable that He who wept by the grave of Lazarus, and who was known among men as a man of sorrows, was unmoved at being so painfully wounded in the house of His friends. His rejection by the nation, which was beloved for the fathers' sake, was a grievous burden for Him to bear.

Isaiah, with prophetic insight, discloses the perfect Servant's innermost thoughts in the face of that rejection. "*I have laboured in vain, I have spent my strength for nothing, and in vain*" (Isa.49:4). While there is no record of these precise words ever having been uttered in public, the language, to put it mildly, certainly seems to be an inward expression of considerable disappointment.

Over against that, we can recall the clear statement of the first song, "He shall not fail nor be discouraged" (Isa.42:4). But, as we have seen, the term used in that song suggests the idea of being knocked out of a race or out of a contest, rather than of being personally immune from disappointment. Whatever the pressures upon Him, and whatever their effect upon others, the Servant will keep right on to the end, He will not fail to finish the course.

The Man of Faith

Even if we allow that our Lord did give expression to a sense of despondency because of His rejection by the people in whom He had invested so much, He never gave way to unbelief. His confidence in God never flagged, and it certainly did not fail. That He maintained the integrity of His trust in God is evident for He went on to say, "*yet surely my judgement [vindication] is with the Lord, and my work [reward] is with my God*" (v.4). In the third song where the unspeakable sufferings endured by the Servant at the hands of His fellows are described, we shall hear more of this same language, the language of faith.

In all this we have much to learn from the Servant King. In particular, we learn that the vital thing in the face of adversity, is not the adversity itself, but our reaction to it. "When He was reviled, He reviled not again; when He suffered, He threatened not." This was not mere resignation and it was more than simple passivity, for we are told, "He committed Himself to Him who judges righteously" (1Pet.2:22,23). Nor was this exercise in vain, because as we have seen, God vindicated Him by raising Him from the dead, and He will vindicate Him again when He appears the second time "to be glorified in His saints, and to be admired in all them who believe" (2Thess.1:10).

The Trial of Faith

At this point it will be helpful to understand two things, (i) that discouragement is not in itself an iniquity, it is rather a human trait or infirmity, and (ii) because He trod the earth before us and experienced our infirmities, the most common of which is a tendency to be discouraged, He is now able to have a fellow feeling with us in all our weaknesses (Hebs.4:15). Moreover, that He was maligned and reviled, that He endured such contradiction of sinners against Himself, and in the end was cast out and put to a shameful death, only serves to underline His true humanity.

For our part we are reassured by the knowledge that He has been where we now are, He has travelled the road we currently tread. Whatever the infirmity pressing on us and whatever the circumstance we are passing through, He has been there in principle, He has been through it. Because of this, the man who is now in the glory can enter with us into our frequent discouragements, and He can adequately meet our need out of His all-sufficient grace.

This is a most important consideration for we have to acknowledge that it is not unusual for God's servants to taste discouragement and despondency. Indeed, this has been the oft repeated lot of some of the most honoured servants of the Lord. But in the hour of trial when the hard times come, we can remember that there is a real man in the presence of God. He is there as our representative. Having identified Himself with us, He now presents Himself as one with whom we can identify.

Thou did'st tread the earth before us,
Thou did'st feel its keenest woe.

A Purpose in Testing

In the ebb and flow of human experience there is an inevitability about disappointments and discouragements. Yet it is in those very circumstances that God accomplishes His gracious purposes and works out His strange designs in our lives. He had very definite purposes in the imprisonment of Joseph, the banishment of Moses, the rejection of David and the fiery trial of Daniel's three friends. And, of course, He had a supreme purpose in the sufferings of our Lord Jesus Christ.

In the course of our own fitful pilgrimage God is still at work, working in us what is wellpleasing in His sight. An isolated incident is seldom the whole story, and in any case, as already stated, what really matters is not the incident itself, but our reaction to it. The important thing for us is not *that* we get out of our troubles; but rather *what* we get out of them. When our hearts are exercised to prove the Lord and His grace, we will always derive spiritual good from our seasons of adversity. The saintly Samuel Rutherford said, "When I find myself in the cellar of affliction, I always look for the wine."

The Triumph of Faith

We are born unto trouble as the sparks fly upward. "For a just man falls seven times, and rises up again" (Prov.24:16). It is not here a matter of falling into sin but of falling into trouble. And yet, whatever form it may take, the trouble is not itself the end; on the contrary it provides us with a further opportunity to prove the Lord and His grace. We should not, therefore, miss the spiritual and very practical lesson enshrined in the perfect Servant's discouragement, for out of it came the subsequent enlargement and the ultimate success of His mission.

Just as myrrh yields its fragrance only when it is crushed, and a seed must first fall into the ground and die, before it can bring forth fruit, so it is through the pressures of the flood, and the fire, that we are conformed to the image of Christ. It was through many distresses that Joseph eventually came to the throne of Egypt, and it is through much tribulation that God's purposes are still accomplished in His people.

Reflecting on the difficult times in one of the Psalms, David said, "You enlarged me when I was in distress," and in another place, "It was good for me that I had been afflicted, that I might learn your statutes" (Psa.4:1;119:71). Evidently David felt himself a better and a stronger man as a result of the trials and difficulties through which God had brought him.

It is of particular interest to note how Paul applied this second song to himself and to his fellow labourers. Did the beloved apostle ever become despondent in his service for the Lord? There was certainly no lack of occasion for him to be discouraged; in afflictions, in necessities, in distresses, in stripes, in imprisonments, in tumults etc. But he did not receive the grace of God in vain. He laid hold of this wonderful pledge of answered prayer in the second song, and appropriated it to his own situation, which he called his accepted time, his day of deliverance. (See 2Cor.6:1-10.)

Enlargement

The key thing to note at this point in our song is that the discouragement of Jehovah's Servant, far from signalling the end of His mission, actually issued in its enlargement. In addition to being God's instrument in the restoration of Israel, He will also become a light to the Gentile nations and the messenger of salvation to the ends of the earth, until, in the end, the whole earth will acknowledge His rule (v.6).

To say that "in all things God is at work for the good of His people" (Rom.8:28 *n.i.v.*) is more than just a cliche, it is the statement of a principle of God's dealings with His people. Its ultimate demonstration will be seen in the perfect Servant. For our part, we must take great care about how we react to the difficult times, because we shall profit from them only to the degree in which we prove God's grace, while passing through them. In this song we are taught to judge nothing before the time, to leave results with God, and to keep before us that all true service rendered in His name, even down to the giving of a cup of cold water in His name, will have its reward.

Our service at times seems so weak and ineffective, and the circumstances of it so difficult. We might be tempted to underestimate its true value in the sight of God. But we shall find strength and comfort by reflecting upon the Servant's reactions to His discouragements. For here in this second song we have a resounding testimony to the man Christ Jesus, and to His constant, humble dependence upon God, when passing through deep waters.

This song, like the first, is followed by a call to universal worship. Besides heaven and earth, the very mountains are summoned to unite in a great ascription of praise. The occasion of this summons, which is still in abeyance, will be the grace and power of God in regathering His people Israel, and in restoring them to the land of promise. Then it shall be said, "*The Lord has comforted His people, and He will have compassion upon His afflicted*" (v.13).

1 Thus saith the Lord: Where is the bill of your mother's divorcement, whom I have put away? Or which of my creditors is it to whom I have sold you? Behold, for your iniquities have ye sold yourselves, and for your transgressions is your mother put away.

2 Wherefore, when I came, was there no man? When I called was there none to answer? Is my hand shortened at all, that it cannot redeem? Or have I no power to deliver? Behold, at my rebuke I dry up the sea, I make the rivers a wilderness; their fish stink, because there is no water, and die for thirst.

3 I clothe the heavens with blackness, and I make sackcloth their covering.

4 The Lord God hath given me the tongue of the learned, that I should know how to speak a word in season to him who is weary; he awakeneth morning by morning; he waketh mine ear to hear like the learned.

5 The Lord God hath opened mine ear, and I was not rebellious, neither turned backward.

6 I gave my back to the smiters, and my cheeks to them that plucked off the hair; I hid not my face from shame and spitting.

7 For the Lord God will help me; therefore shall I not be confounded; Therefore have I set my face like a flint, and I know that I shall not be ashamed.

8 He is near who justifieth me. Who will contend with me? Let us stand together. Who is mine adversary? Let him come near to me.

9 Behold, the Lord God will help me. Who is he that shall condemn me? Lo, they shall all grow old like a garment; the moth shall eat them up.

10 Who is among you that feareth the Lord, that obeyeth the voice of his servant, that walketh in darkness, and hath no light? Let him trust in the name of the Lord, and stay upon his God.

11 Behold, all ye that kindle a fire, that compass yourselves about with sparks: walk in the light of your fire, and in the sparks that ye have kindled. This shall ye have of mine hand; ye shall lie down in sorrow.

3rd Servant Song: Isaiah 50:1-11

The *Third Song*

The third song deals with the reasons behind Israel's present dispersion, and points on, by implication, to a future recovery. It also gives unique insights into Messiah's sufferings at the hands of the chosen people.

The Calamities of Israel

You have sold yourselves... (v.1)

The best introduction to this third song is found in the closing verses of the previous chapter. The call to worship which follows the second song concludes with these words, " ... *the Lord has comforted His people, and will have mercy on His afflicted*" (Isa.49:13). But this raises some very pertinent questions. If this be true, why is it that Israel is still scattered? Why have the high ideals of the kingdom not yet materialised?

Added to this we have Israel's complaint in the next verse: "*But Zion said, The Lord has forsaken me, and my Lord has forgotten me*" (Isa.49:14). The clear inference is of a great divide between Israel's promised renewal and her present state. This third song looks behind the scenes and helps to explain Israel's predicament, which remains to the present day.

That it is not unusual for creatures to blame their adversity on the Creator was first demonstrated in the garden of Eden. (See Gen.3.) But through Isaiah the Lord totally rejected any implied charge. The present condition of His people is not because of some failure on His part. Israel is ever before Him, she is graven on the palms of His hands. Why, His love for Israel surpasses even that of a nursing mother for her child (Isa.49:15,16).

The third song goes to the heart of the matter. It highlights the treatment meted out to Messiah at the time of His first advent. The callous spurning of her Redeemer, the Holy One, is the reason, behind every other reason, for Israel's national calamities. If Israel had only known, in the day of her visitation, the things that belonged to her peace! But now they are hidden from her.

The Diaspora

From the end of the monarchy through to the second advent, two dispersions followed by two recoveries will sum up Israel's total story. Very largely, though not exclusively, the second part of Isaiah's prophecy looks forward to the second recovery, when the present, long drawn out dispersion, or diaspora will be brought to an end. It envisages Israel's regathering in the last days. It even begins with the comfort with which the Lord will, in the end, comfort His people. (See Isa.40:1,2.)

Ezekiel lived and worked during the time of the first dispersion. His ministry was to his own people who were enduring the rigours of captivity in Babylon. (See Psa.137:1.) At times, however, his words seemed to take account of a further and greater dispersion when the people would be scattered abroad among all the nations of the earth. But Ezekiel predicted that even then a remnant would be preserved, and would ultimately be restored to the promised land.

His prediction of this was very precise. He said, "Thus saith the Lord God: Although I have cast them afar off among the nations, and although I have scattered them among the countries, yet will I be to them as a little sanctuary in the countries where they shall come. Therefore say ... I will even gather you from the people, and assemble you out of the countries where ye have been scattered, and I will give you the land of Israel" (Ezk.11:16, 17).

The Certificate of Divorce

Probing into the background of this second dispersion, the third song begins with two rather unusual questions. The first is this, "*Where is the bill of your mother's divorce?*" (v.1) In legislating for divorce, Moses had established a sequence of steps which, when completed, would have made the reconstruction of the original marriage impossible. One of those steps was the issuing of a certificate, or bill of divorce. (See Deut.24:1-4.)

Isaiah's reasoning seems to be that while the nation of Israel (*your mother*) has been put away (*divorced*) (v.1), the absence of any certificate, as the question implies, means that the breakdown between Israel and her God is not deemed irretrievable. The possibility of a reconcilation at some future date is not ruled out. In his time, the apostle Paul would argue powerfully that while Israel has been *set aside*, Israel has not been *cast off*. (See Rom.11:1,2.)

The other question at the beginning of the song is not unlike the first. "*To which of my creditors is it to whom I have sold you?*" It was another rhetorical question and an immediate answer was given, "*Behold ... you have sold yourselves*" (v.1). Israel had been uniquely chosen to serve God, and was often referred to as His servant, but she had sold herself to become the slave of other masters.

Here again, there is no indication that this situation was irredeemable. The law simply decreed that persons in this position were deprived of any legal rights or claims. It did not rule out the possibility of the position itself being restored. The widow, who lived in the time of Elisha, and whose creditor had come to take away her two sons to be slaves, is an instance of such a restoration. (See 2Kings 4:1-7.)

The Cause of the Second Dispersion

But Isaiah went further. He stated in quite categorical terms, the reasons behind both the divorce and the slavery. "*Behold, for your iniquities have you sold yourselves, and for your transgressions is your mother put away*" (v.1). In a later reference, the prophet underlined the seriousness of Israel's sin, "Your iniquities have separated between you and your God, and your sins have hidden His face from you, that He will not hear" (Isa.59:2).

From the beginning, this was the effect that sin had on man in his relations with God. And it was no different in the case of the chosen people. Nor could it have been, for "God is no respecter of persons; but in every nation he that fears Him, and works righteousness, is accepted with Him" (Acts10:34,35). In view of this, the real cause of Israel's present spiritual condition, and the culpability for it, is made clear in this song.

More than Idolatry

But the prophet put a finer point on Israel's offence. For two issues of very great importance lay behind the charge: (i) Israel's iniquity was corporate, her transgression was national; and (ii) of even more consequence, the evil was not just a simple return to the idolatry of the pre-captivity era, but it involved the actual casting out of her Redeemer. She scorned her long promised Messiah, the one to whom all her prophets had borne witness. Standing in her midst was one whom she knew not. He was great David's greater Son, and in crass unbelief she cried out, "We have no king but Caesar." Individuals, here and there, did recognise Him and gave Him their allegiance, but the nation's official verdict on its King was this, "We will not have this man to reign over us" (Luke 19:14).

Messiah had openly and plainly presented Himself to the people. He was heralded by the forerunner, and accredited by the fulfilment of the many and varied prophecies that had gone before, but they would not have Him. He appealed to the nation's conscience in tones of tenderest love. He even wept over their city, but such compassion did not evoke a proper response in their hearts.

With spectacular precision, in this third song, Isaiah foretold the attitude of his people in the day of their visitation. He reported in advance the Servant's overtures: how He looked for a man but there was none, and how He called for a response, but no answer came. "*Wherefore, when I came, was there no man? When I called, there was none to answer*" (v.2).

The Second Man, the Last Adam

The first Adam might have been the man, but he had failed. And so a promise was given of a future redeemer. He would not come from the serried ranks of angels or archangels; He would be a man, born of a woman. God waited four thousand years for humanity to produce such a man, and two thousand years for the seed of Abraham to do so, but all was in vain. The deficiency was highlighted by Ezekiel, "*I sought for a man* among them, that should make up the hedge, and stand in the gap before me for the land, that I should not destroy it, *but I found none*" (Ezk.22:30). And then in the fulness of time, God sent forth His Son. The Lord Jesus was born of a woman, of the seed of Abraham and of the seed of David.

The long awaited man had at last appeared, He was the second man and the last Adam. When He came we are told, "He saw that there was no man, and wondered that there was no intercessor: therefore His arm brought salvation unto Him; and His righteousness, it sustained Him" (Isa.59:16). Again through the same prophet we hear Him say, "And I looked, and there was none to help; and I wondered that there was none to uphold: therefore my own arm brought salvation unto me; and my fury it upheld me" (Isa.63:5).

Israel's leaders knew well the scripture which said, "A man shall be an hiding place from the wind, a covert from the tempest; like rivers of water in a dry place, like the shadow of a great rock in a weary land" (Isa.32:2). But when that man finally presented himself, they esteemed Him a man of sorrows, and simply refused to recognise Him. This resulted in the wife of Jehovah becoming as a divorced woman; and Israel, His servant, becoming as a slave in the service of an enemy.

Lo-ammi - *not* my people

Twice over, in our song, the prophet uses the expression *put away* to describe Israel's present position. While recognising the temporary nature of this state, we must not forget that the state itself is a divine judgement upon the people whom God had chosen. Their putting away, or setting aside, means that Israel had become *Lo-ammi*, i.e. *not my people* (Hosea1:9). This solemn decree created a situation that has now been drawn out to around two thousand years.

And yet, this long period was not unforeseen by the prophets. Hosea went on to say, "The children of Israel shall abide *many days* without a king, and without a prince, and without a sacrifice, and without an image, and without an ephod, and without teraphim." But the prophet is not without hope for he added, "Afterward shall the children of Israel return, and seek the Lord, their God ... in the latter days" (Hosea 3:4).

Hosea' reference to the many things that identified Israel, in an outward way at any rate, as the chosen people of God is interesting. It is quite astonishing that across the centuries since the time of the first dispersion and the beginning of the *Times of the Gentiles*, Israel has never regained those outward symbols. And her rejection of Messiah simply had the effect of perpetuating the loss.

The Cloud

In somewhat dramatic language, Ezekiel described the withdrawal of the glory cloud from over the temple in Jerusalem. The cloud had been the most prominent outward sign of God's presence among His people. The prophet saw the cloud move first from over the temple to a new position over the city, then it moved again to a position over the mount of Olives, before finally disappearing altogether. (See Ezk.10.)

The Temple

The temple itself, but always without its centrepiece, the ark of the covenant, remained for a further five hundred years, until it was destroyed by the Roman armies under Titus in AD70. Jesus had predicted of the temple, "There shall not be left here one stone standing upon another, that shall not be thrown down" (Matt.24:2). Any pilgrim to Jerusalem today can see how that prophesy was fulfilled in its utmost detail. Yet at the close of his prophecy Ezekiel foretells the restoration of the temple and the re-appearing of the glory cloud.

The Throne of David

Another symbol of Israel's favoured position was the throne of David. Its existence is a matter of history; that it is not in place today is a matter of fact. But both parts of scripture affirm that the Davidic dynasty will be re-established at the time of the second advent. (See Amos 9:11&Acts15:16.) To transfer David's Jerusalem throne to heaven in some kind of spiritual sense, as some are inclined to do, is a rather arbitrary use of the scriptures. In any case, the Lord Jesus is not now seated upon David's throne in Heaven. His own report is, "I am set down with my Father on *His* throne" (Rev.3:21).

In his celebrated sermon on the day of Pentecost, the apostle Peter proclaimed, in no uncertain terms, the resurrection of Jesus Christ from the dead. Significantly, he argued his case from what David had said in the sixteenth psalm, "Therefore, being a prophet, and knowing that God had sworn with an oath unto him, that of the fruit of his loins, according to the flesh, He would raise up Christ to sit on his throne; he seeing this before spoke of the resurrection of Christ ... " (Acts 2:30-32).

His essential thesis, plainly stated, was this, 'Christ had to rise from the dead, because a dead messiah could not sit on David's throne.' And since Christ is risen, the resurrection has cleared the way for the fulfilment of Gabriel's word to the virgin mother, "And the Lord God shall give unto Him the throne of His father, David. And He shall reign over the house of Jacob forever; and of His kingdom there shall be no end" (Luke 1:32,33).

The exercise of this government by Mary's Son was very much in Isaiah's vision when he spoke of Messiah as the child to be born, and the son to be given. He went on, "Of the increase of His government and peace there shall be no end, upon the throne of David, and upon his kingdom, to order it, and to establish it, with justice and with righteousness from henceforth even forever. The zeal of the Lord of hosts will perform this" (Isa 9:6,7).

The *Third Song*

The Calamities of Israel (Contd.)

Is my hand shortened ?

Israel was chosen to be the vehicle through which God would bear witness to Himself among the nations of the earth. The Hebrew people were intended to have a primary role in God's governmental purposes worldwide. In all their various dominions, the nations were to be ruled and governed with reference to the nation of Israel.

The nations in our contemporary world would do well to ponder the background to Israel's long dispersion. When obedient to the government of God, Israel found blessing, but disobedience always brought cursing. And this principle is relevant to both men and nations in our own day. Let us not imagine, even for a moment, that the living God is irrelevant to our national life.

Several scriptures make plain Israel's intended role, as the focus of God's government on the earth. "When the Most High divided to the nations their inheritance, He set the bounds of the people according to the number of the children of Israel. For the Lord's portion is His people; Jacob is the lot of His inheritance" (Deut 32:8,9). And again, "The Lord has avowed [owned] you this day to be His peculiar people ... to make you high above all nations whom He has made, in praise, and in name, and in honour" (Deut.26:18,19).

Two Ideals

(i) A witness against idolatry

God's choice of Israel was moral as well as political. Two quite specific ideals lay behind it. In the first place, Israel was to be a witness to the nations against the evils of idolatry. Since Satan is the prime mover behind all forms of idolatry, it follows that idolatry is abominable in God's sight. In all probability, Abraham was an idolator in Mesopotamia when the God of glory appeared to him. But God called him out and away from the worship of his idols, to become the father of the Hebrew race.

Later, when the law was given at Sinai, the worship of any god save Jehovah was emphatically ruled out. The first commandment said, "You shall have no other gods before me" (Deut.5:7). This requirement was also a recurring theme and a primary emphasis in the ministry of the prophets. For example, Isaiah reminded his hearers, "You are my witnesses, saith the Lord, that I am God" (Isa.43:12).

(ii) A people whose God is the Lord

The second ideal was that Israel should be a pattern or model to the nations, showing them that the secret of happiness and prosperity, lay in a right relationship with Jehovah. Just two months out from the house of bondage the Lord said to His redeemed ones, "If you will obey my voice indeed, and keep my covenant, then you shall be a peculiar treasure unto me above all people; for all the earth is mine" (Ex.19:5). And again, "If you will indeed obey ... and do all that I speak; then I will be an enemy unto your enemies, and an adversary unto your adversaries" (Ex.23:22).

Some time later He added, "If you walk in my statutes and keep my commandments and do them; then I will give you rain in due season, and the land shall yield her increase, and the trees of the field shall yield their fruit. Your threshing shall reach unto the vintage, and the vintage shall reach unto the sowing time; and you shall eat your bread to the full, and dwell in your land safely ... And I will set my tabernacle among you: and my soul shall not abhor you. And I will walk among you, and will be your God, and you will be my people" (Lev.26:3-12).

With these and many other similar promises behind her, Israel was intended to relate peacefully to all the nations of the earth, without being dependent on any of them. Moses, the great law-giver had told his people, "You shall lend unto many nations, but you shall not borrow; and you shall reign over many nations but they shall not reign over you" (Deut.15:6). Israel's dependence would be on God's arm alone.

Hopes and Expectations

There was an eager anticipation of these things at the end of the wilderness wanderings. In his parting words to his people Moses said, "Happy are you, O Israel! Who is like unto you, O people saved by the Lord, the shield of your help ... the sword of your excellency? Your enemies shall be found liars unto you, and you shall tread upon their high places" (Deut.33:29).

But the nearest Israel ever attained to this level of blessing, was in the halcyon days of David and Solomon. When King David heard the terms of God's covenant, he sat before the Lord, and said, "What one nation in the earth is like your people, Israel, whom God went to redeem to be His own people ... for your people Israel, did you make your own people forever; and you, Lord, became their God" (I Chron.17:21,22).

Following David's death, Solomon, his son, reigned in his stead. Those were times of abundant peace and prosperity, times that have not been equalled in the long story of the human race. "God gave Solomon wisdom and exceeding much understanding, and largeness of heart, even as the sand that is on the seashore ... And there came from all peoples to hear the wisdom of Solomon, from all kings of the earth, who had heard of his wisdom" (1Kings 4:29,34).

Israel's Apostasy

But the enjoyment of this peace and prosperity was always conditioned upon Israel's continuing subjection to the Lord, and this simply did not materialise. The nations had degraded the knowledge of the true and living God. They fell into idolatry and made images like corruptible man, and birds, and four-footed beasts, and creeping things. (See Rom.1:20-23.) And with the passing of time Israel became like the nations. "They mingled among the heathen, and learned their works. And they served their idols, which were a snare unto them. Yea, they sacrificed their sons and their daughters unto [demons]" (Psa.106:35-37).

In Solomon's old age, apostasy was already in evidence throughout the nation, and a severe warning was given that disobedience would be followed by discipline. And so it came to pass, for shortly after Solomon's death the kingdom was divided. When Rehoboam, his son, came to the throne, the ten northern tribes, thereafter called Israel, broke away from the two southern tribes now known as Judah. The one nation had become two. And to this day, that division has not been healed.

The history of the ten tribes is a dark and lamentable tale of departure and apostasy, with scarcely any remission, until they were eventually swept away from their land by the king of Assyria. Of the many wicked things they did to provoke the Lord to anger the most prominent was their lapse into idolatry, "They served idols, of which the Lord had said unto them, You shall not do this thing." (See 2Kings17:11,12.)

The story of the two southern tribes was only a little better, until, in the days of Zedekiah, the last of the kings to sit upon the throne of David and Solomon at Jerusalem, they too were carried away. Nebuchadnezzar brought them down to Babylon where they remained in captivity for seventy years (2Chron.36:20,21). At the end of that rather fraught period, a remnant of the people returned to the land. We have called this the first recovery. Its purpose was, as we have pointed out, that the people should be in the land to herald Messiah's first advent.

Messiah's rejection

But the painful record of His people's rebellion reached its high point when they refused their long awaited Messiah. This is the issue so heavily underscored in the opening part of the third song: the rejection of the anointed king. The putting away or setting aside of the people, and their scattering among the nations, was the immediate and direct consequence of Messiah's rejection.

The world to which the Lord Jesus came was an incredibly hostile place. For Him that hostility reached its high point at the time of His trial before Pilate. With detailed precision, Luke, the evangelist, catalogued the enmity that confronted Him in the judgement hall. When Pilate said, "I find no fault in this man, "the chief priests became the *more fierce* ... They stood up and *vehemently* accused Him ... and Herod, with his men of war, *treated Him with contempt, and mocked Him*" (Luke 23:5,10,11).

The people who did these things were not barbarians, the sort of people who would simply murder their mentors. They were the leaders of the most cultivated and civilised community on the face of the earth. Their forebears had been honourable attendants in the court of King Solomon. Moreover, they were well instructed in their own sacred writings, and they even claimed to be looking for the coming one. On the face of it, and with the objectivity that two millennia can give, it seems incredible that the chosen people should have behaved in the way they did.

The Core Issue

When scorned in the camp of Saul, the youthful David asked his brothers, "Is there not a cause?" Of course there was a cause, both in David's day and also in Messiah's. In the case of the latter, the cause centred in His claim that He was the Son of God. This had been the issue, that eclipsed all other issues from the beginning of His ministry. We are well informed about His claims, and how the Jews responded to them. For example, when He said, "*Before Abraham was, I am*. Then took they up stones to cast at Him." Similarly on another occasion when He claimed, "*I and my Father are one*, then the Jews took up stones again to stone Him" (John 8:58,59; 10:30,31).

If His claims were false then He was a blasphemer, and according to their law He had to die. On this pretext they delivered Him to Pilate who, in turn, delivered Him to be crucified. In the event, His claims were uniquely demonstrated to be true, for on the third day God raised Him from the dead. The apostolic witness is that He was

"Declared to be the Son of God with power, according to the spirit of holiness, by the resurrection from the dead" (Rom.1:4).

True, for them this was still in the future. But they were without excuse for they had incontrovertible testimony placed before them. They had the witness both of His words and of His works. And if this had not been enough, they had also seen the Roman Governor point Him out and say, "Behold, the man!" And again, "he [Pilate] said unto the Jews, Behold your King!" (John 19:5,14) But even when their own scriptures were quoted to them by the Roman authorities, they closed their minds and would not believe on Him. At the time of His showing unto Israel, the chosen people were seized by an obstinate unbelief that simply would not allow them to recognise their king.

The Political Card

Of course, we must take on board the hard fact that those Jews were in the land at the deference of their Gentile masters. While this was true of the people as a whole, it was a matter of special gravity to their leaders. The latter had a fairly generous deal with the Romans. They lived quite comfortable lives in Jerusalem, and they enjoyed a large degree of autonomy. They virtually ran their own affairs. The single issue that would put everything in jeopardy was civil unrest.

That the possibility of civil disturbance weighed heavily with them is clear from their own council minutes! "Then gathered the chief priests and the Pharisees a council, and said, What do we? For this man does many miracles. If we let Him alone, all men will believe on Him; and the Romans shall come and take away both our place and nation" (John11:47,48). Their fear was that the popularity of Jesus among the common people, who heard Him gladly, would lead to civil commotion, and that this, in turn, would undermine their entire position.

There were other additional reasons as well. We have noted that the coming of the promised one was seen by the prophets in the context of two advents, and that the prophets themselves could not always or easily discern between the sufferings of Messiah on the one hand, and His glory on the other. Moreover, there is much evidence to suggest that the expectation of the people at the time, living as they were under the Roman yoke, was that Messiah, when He came, would present Himself as their deliverer in a political sense. He would break the detested political yoke and lead them in triumph over all their foes. In a word, He would destroy the Roman overlordship.

Through Disciples' Eyes

We have confirmation for this view in the two travellers on the road to Emmaus. This was the underlying concern in their response to the stranger who had joined them in their journey, and whom they failed to recognise. They were obviously dejected and even disillusioned, and they said, "We hoped that it had been He who should have redeemed Israel" (Luke 24:21). Although they were disciples of Christ, they had evidently failed to grasp the significance of the things that were happening.

In their confusion they had concluded that the action of their rulers, and of the Roman authorities, had proved that Jesus was not their Messiah, nor was He Israel's king. Apart from any other consideration, He had not put up the slightest resistance, as might have been expected of a national deliverer. But the stranger quickly corrected their thinking. He did so by demonstrating from the scriptures, that His death was a cardinal part of a total strategy. It was essential for the redemption of His people Israel.

The Apostles

The same thinking was true of the apostles whom He had chosen. He spent the forty days following His resurrection instructing them in the kingdom of God. But the only question they wanted an answer to was this, "Lord, wilt thou at this time restore again the kingdom to Israel?" (Acts 1:6) It was not a foolish question, nor did He rebuke them for asking it. He simply replied that the question of timing was a secret in the counsels of God.

In the event, a transitional period was about to begin. Because the King had been refused, the messianic kingdom was in process of postponement. In its place God was about to launch a wholly new enterprise, the calling out of the Church. That transitional period, which is still running its course, is the background theme of the book of Acts, and we should read that book with this always in mind. The question raised by the apostles, therefore, was not answered by a plain yes or no, it was simply set aside. In the same way, national Israel too has been set aside.

By putting these things together we are able to rationalize, in some measure, Messiah's rejection. They were looking for a man of war, but He came in lowly form, taking a disciple's place and assuming a servant's habit. He was a man full of grace and truth, consecrated to do His Father's will, and they failed to recognise Him. Of course, if we bring into the equation a working of Satan, we can see a further dimension to our Lord's rejection by His people. But to add insult to injury, their unbelief led them into all sorts of excesses. They ploughed upon His back and pulled the hair from His cheeks. They spat in His face and covered Him with shame (Isa.50:6).

The Promised Recovery

We need to stress again, however, that Israel's present condition is not permanent. Paul wrote "Blindness in part is happened unto Israel, *until* the fulness of the Gentiles be come in" (Rom.11:25), and to that we can add the earlier statements of Jesus. In one instance He said, "Your house is left unto you desolate. For I say unto you, you shall not see me henceforth, *till* you shall say, Blessed is He that comes in the name of the Lord" (Matt.23:38,39). Again He declared, "Jerusalem shall be trodden down by the Gentiles, *until* the times of the Gentiles be fulfilled" (Luke 21:24).

What Isaiah said:

When the astonishing renewal of national Israel takes place, it will not be achieved by evolutionary processes or by grandiose schemes of man's devising, but by the appearing in glory of Israel's Messiah at His second advent. Until then, the world's statesmen will continue to hold their conferences, and to sign their peace accords, but experience has proved that their achievements, even at their best, are very limited. In striking contrast to all such things, and in clear and unambiguous language, Isaiah predicted the coming day of glory when the outcasts of Israel will be assembled, and the dispersed of Judah will be gathered from the four corners of the earth. (See Isa.11:11.)

In another reference the same prophet went on to announce, "It shall come to pass in that day, that the remnant of Israel, and such as have escaped of the house of Jacob, shall no more again lean upon him who smote them, but shall lean upon the Lord, the Holy One of Israel, in truth. The remnant shall return, even the remnant of Jacob, unto the mighty God. For though your people Israel be as the sand of the sea, yet a remnant of them shall return" (Isa.10:20-22).

What Moses said:

Towards the end of his life, and centuries before Isaiah was born, Moses had predicted such a regathering of his people whom he foresaw scattered among the nations: "And it shall come to pass, when all these things are come upon you, the blessing and the curse, which I have set before you, and you shall call them to mind among *all the nations*, to which the Lord your God has driven you, and shall return unto the Lord your God, and obey His voice, that then the Lord your God will turn your captivity, and have compassion upon you, and will return and gather you from *all nations* where the Lord your God has scattered you" (Deut.30:1-3).

What the great law-giver evidently had in view was more than a merely physical regathering. That future recovery will be energised by a dynamic spiritual revival. For Moses went on to say, "And the Lord your God will circumcise your heart, and the heart of your seed, to love the Lord your God with all your heart, and with all your soul, that you may live" (Deut.30:6).

Zechariah testified to this spiritual dynamic as well. "And I will pour upon the house of David and upon the inhabitants of Jerusalem, the Spirit of grace and of supplications; and they shall look upon me whom they have pierced, and they shall mourn for him, as one mourneth for his only son, and shall be in bitterness for him, as one is in bitterness for his firstborn" (Zech.12:10).

Thus it will come to pass. Through a national humiliation, induced by a mighty outpouring of the Spirit of God, Israel will be brought back again to the Lord, and to the purpose for which she had been chosen at the beginning. And in association with the Messiah she once rejected, Israel will be restored to the land of promise. She will become what she was intended to be, a vessel for the manifestation of the glory of God in the earth. And then, as in the days of David and Solomon, she will again take her place at the head of the nations.

The *Third Song*

The Afflictions of Messiah

I dry up the sea ... I was not rebellious (v.2)

Some consider the Father to be the speaker in the first three verses of this chapter, and that the Son speaks only in the verses following. However, it is unnecessary to be dogmatic on this point, for there is probably a deliberate movement between the two persons which in itself serves to remind us again of the doctrine of the trinity.

The speaker certainly claims for Himself creatorial powers: He says, "*I clothe the heavens with blackness, and I make sackcloth their covering*" (v.3). In the previous verse He makes reference, respectively, to how He dried up the Red Sea and the river Jordan. The speaker, therefore, can be none other than the God of creation, the Holy One of Israel.

But since He also describes Himself as the one who came and called for an answer, and found none (v.2), we conclude that the speaker is our Lord Jesus Christ who came unto His own. If this is so, then we have here another covert reminder that the Jesus of the New Testament, and the Jehovah of the Old Testament, is one and the same. The nature of the Holy Trinity is such that the Son could become a man without ceasing to be God. And this is what He did when, in the mystery of the incarnation, He appeared among men to accomplish the divine counsels.

The Suffering Servant

Untold suffering was predicted for the Redeemer when the promise of His coming was first given to Adam and Eve, prior to their expulsion from Eden. In bruising the serpent's head, the Redeemer's own heel would be bruised. (See Gen.3:15.) The prediction was certainly justified by its fulfilment, for more than any other, the Lord Jesus, our blessed Redeemer, is the man who has seen affliction.

In the previous song we had more than a hint of the anguish He endured. This third song goes further, and describes in graphic detail the sufferings and afflictions that were involved in His mission to the messianic nation. The growing intensity of those sufferings, and their climax in the cross, is recorded in both the third and fourth songs.

Both songs testify to the sufferings He endured as the central feature of Messiah's experience during His passage through this vale of tears. The two songs, however, require us to distinguish with great care between the many things He suffered during His life on earth, and His atoning sufferings.

The song before us specifically calls attention to the intensely personal nature of the things He suffered. We read of the Servant's *tongue*. We hear Him speak of *my ear*, *my back*, *my cheeks* and of *my face*. The emotive terms He used are certainly arresting. He speaks of the smiting, the plucking off of the hair, the shame and the spitting. A helpful way to analyse this song is to focus on these many personal references.

The Master becomes the Disciple

The disciples who were called by the Lord Jesus, that they might be with Him, named Him their Master and Lord, and He accepted their address. He told them, "You call me Master and Lord; and you say well; for so I am" (John13:13). But here, in this third song, the Master Himself takes the place of a disciple, and does so of His own volition (v.4).

We should note carefully that this verse begins with the *tongue of the learned* and concludes with the *ear of the learned.* The word translated *learned* in the *a.v.* is rendered *instructed* in the *n.i.v.; scholar* might even better supply the meaning, and some have preferred *disciple.* The latter seems to convey the sense best, for it emphasises the principle of discipleship, and lays down the rule that having a disciple's ear is an essential prerequisite to having a disciple's tongue.

Day by day the Saviour's ear was opened to hear God's word, and this in turn equipped Him to speak an appropriate and seasonable word to those who are designated *the weary.* At the same time, obedience to that word brought Him into direct conflict with others, who became His enemies wrongfully, and at whose hands He was to suffer unspeakable anguish.

The Seasonable Word

Early in His ministry, the Servant spelt out the very essence of that *seasonable word* to the people of Nazareth. Paying a return visit to His native city, Jesus stood up in the synagogue and began to read, "The Spirit of the Lord is upon me, because He has anointed me to preach the gospel to the poor; He has sent me to heal the brokenhearted, to preach deliverance to the captives, and recovering of sight to the blind, to set at liberty them that are bruised, to preach the acceptable year of the Lord" (Luke 4:18, 19).

He was reading directly from Isaiah, and we should note the profoundly significant point at which He closed the book and sat down. Had He read on, the next phrase says: "And the day of vengeance of our God." (See Isa.61:1,2.) The Saviour had come to announce the acceptable year of the Lord, and so he stopped reading in the middle of the sentence and closed the book. In the goodness of God the acceptable year has been extended to the present time.

When the book is opened again it will be to announce the day of vengeance. We should not overlook a very meaningful play on words at this point, vengeance is for a day, while the good news is for a year. It has been well said that judgement is God's strange work.

In the meantime, to the poor, the captive, the blind and the bruised, and to all who feel the burden of sin, the perfect Servant's word is always seasonable, it is always relevant. Moreover, no matter how varied the weary ones may consider their needs to be, the word itself is always the same; it is the word of the truth of the gospel. While there may be different aspects to it, there is only one gospel. It is the everlasting gospel and for this very reason it is always in season.

A Word to the Weary

Weariness in one form or another, has marked the human race ever since the fall. There is the physical weariness of the labourer and the mental weariness of those whose intellectual resources are exhausted. Happily, in most cases, such may easily and quickly find renewal. But there is another kind of weariness upon men. As a result of the fall, men still labour and are heavy laden, they still groan under the burdens of guilt and care, and apart from some temporary relief, they find no real remedy on any purely human level.

At the time of the first advent, the Jews were labouring under the burden of a law which they could not keep, and the Gentiles under the oppressive burdens of idolatrous and pagan religions. Then Jesus came "A light to lighten the Gentiles, and the glory of His people, Israel" (Luke 2:32). He came to give light to them that sit in darkness and in the shadow of death. He came to roll back the frontiers of darkness and to bring the light of the glorious gospel to bear upon men's lives.

The gospel is the good news of a special kind of rest, a rest that is not dependent upon outward circumstances. It comes to us in the form of a direct and personal invitation from the Saviour Himself: "Come unto me, all you who labour and are heavy laden, and I will give you rest. Take my yoke upon you, and learn of me; for I am meek and lowly in heart, and you shall find rest unto your souls" (Matt.11:28,29). The only required qualification on our part is an acknowledgment of our need.

The chosen nation

Distinguishing between the classes and conditions of people among whom the Lord was found when He was here on earth is a very interesting study. The phrase *"him who is weary"* probably refers in the first place to the chosen nation, for we know that His mission was primarily to the house of Israel. However, Israel did not recognise the day of her visitation.

A Remnant within Israel

The phrase may even have a much narrower significance. For our Lord's immediate lot was among those described as "the saints ... and the excellent in whom is all my delight" (Psa.16:3). The reference here seems to point to the godly remnant in Israel at that time. They are referred to as "those who looked for redemption in Jerusalem" (Luke 2:38). God has never left Himself without a witness, and even at that time there was a remnant of people who truly loved the Lord and who thought upon His name.

That little flock was ready and waiting to receive the Redeemer. Among them were Simeon and Anna, as well as those who ministered to Him of their substance. There were others besides, such as those who came to anoint His body at the time of His death. The phrase, *"him who is weary"* probably embraces them all, for this tiny remnant was in great distress. Together they found solace and strength as they hung upon His every word. They, more than any others, must have marvelled at the gracious words which proceeded out of His mouth.

Every Creature

But today, the term *"him who is weary"* has a much larger application. For the gospel is now being proclaimed to every creature under heaven. And the weary in this context are those who have found that the best this old world can offer is only a broken cistern. They are the people who, under every sun, have made the life changing discovery that "love and life and lasting joy" are found in Christ alone.

Following His resurrection the Lord Jesus commissioned the disciples to, "Go into all the world, and preach the gospel to every creature" (Mk.16:15). Across all the years since then, and in every generation, a great army of devoted messengers have responded, and continue to respond, to that commission. They report back that where the gospel is received, darkness and superstition give way to light and hope; and weary souls find rest and peace through believing.

The Disciple's 'Know How'

The prophet also recognised that in a unique sense this Servant possessed the *'know how'* or the ability to speak such a word (v.4). This calls to mind what was said of the Herald in the previous song. "The Lord has called me from the womb ... He has made my mouth like a sharp sword" (Isa.49:1,2). Clearly the sharp sword is a symbol for His speech, which was always with power.

Nicodemus

Several examples of this *know how* have been preserved from His ministry. How appropriate was the word He spoke to Nicodemus, who came to Him by night. "Except a man be born of water and of the Spirit, he cannot enter into the kingdom of God" (John 3:5). It was a word calculated to arrest the man's attention and to meet his need. It cast him back on the scriptures of the prophets, with which he was so familiar. Being a master in Israel his mind would instinctively turn to the washing of regeneration and the renewing of the Holy Spirit spoken of by the prophet Ezekiel. (See Ezk.36.25-27.)

The Woman of Samaria

An entirely different word was called for in His next encounter. And so pertinent was what He said to the woman of Samaria, she was convicted of her sin and brought to acknowledge her need. Then He gave her a word of promise that surely spoke solace to her weary heart (John.4:14). The reality of her faith became manifest in her works, and she became a witness to other needy souls. Her message to them was simple "Come, see a man, who told me all things that ever I did. Is not this the Christ?" (John 4:29)

It is just here that the problem arises for us. We have the gospel, the seasonable word, but our attempts to communicate it are often clumsy and leave much to be desired. Too often, we only succeed in alienating the very people we are seeking to win. We seem to have a limitless capacity for saying the wrong thing, or perhaps the right thing in a wrong way. But the Servant's *know-how* embraced both the message itself, and the manner of its delivery.

Even Moses, the great lawgiver, erred at this very point, and for his error he was prohibited from leading his people into Canaan. "He spoke unadvisedly with his lips" (Psa.106:33). Being once more without water, the people had fallen again to murmuring. Moses, as was his custom, turned to the Lord and was told what to do. But what he did, while it was a prefectly natural reaction, was a complete distortion of the character of God. There was no word of reproach or rebuke, no trace of recrimination in what the Lord had said, but this was not reflected in Moses speech. (See Num.20:10.)

All who engage in home visitation will know best how diverse are the needs of weary souls today. They will also know that to be bearers of a truly seasonable word they must be like Isaiah's Servant. They must maintain an ear attuned to hear for themselves a word from the Lord. That word, in turn, will become in the ears of those to whom they minister, as refreshing rain to a parched earth. One of *Frances Ridley Havergal's* much loved hymns begins with two lines that encapsulate this idea.

Lord speak to me, that I may speak
In living echoes of thy tone.

This is not so much a prayer that we might simply and effectively preach God's word, it is rather a prayer that we might, in attitude and in tone, communicate something of the Lord Himself in all our proclamations. It petitions the Lord that we might have a little of the *'know how'* of the Servant King. That we might know not only *what to say* but also *how and when to say it*, for there is a time to speak and there is a time to keep silent.

This '*know how*' embraces both the manner and method of our communication. A sympathetic word will be of no avail if it is conveyed in a manner that is cold and unfriendly. We must learn to draw alongside weary souls with the sensitivity and compassion of Him who will not break the bruised reed nor quench the smoking flax. The hallmark of every true servant of Christ is this ability to minister with compassion, as his master did, seasonable words to those who are weary and oppressed.

The *Third Song*

The Afflictions of Messiah (Contd.)

He wakens my ear (v.4)

Throughout the scriptures attention is called to the fact that it was by the hearing of the ear that people became aware of the mind of God. We are told "faith comes by hearing, and hearing by the word of God" (Rom.10:17). A close relationship between the tongue and the ear is well established in the physical realm. And as in the physical, so it is in the spiritual, a dumb person is also often deaf.

The function of hearing in a spiritual sense, therefore, is a matter of immense importance. And herein lies the key to developing the '*know how*' of which our song speaks. The ability to speak a seasonable word to weary souls is not a matter of human formula or of professional technique. It is rather an art whose primary secret lies in acquiring a disciple's tongue through the cultivation of a disciple's ear.

The Hearing Ear

A moment's reflection on a familiar Old Testament incident will enable us to appreciate the importance of the ear in spiritual things. The occasion we have in mind was when Isaac, his intention being to bless Esau, was deceived into blessing Jacob instead. It was an occasion that brought all the old man's senses into play. First, there was his failing *sight,* for his eyes were dim that he could not see.

Then there was his sense of *taste* and of *smell*; he requested Esau to bring him venison, savoury food such as he loved. Finally, there was *feeling* and *hearing*, for when Jacob stood disguised before him, Isaac felt his hands, and said, "The voice is Jacob's voice, but the hands are the hands of Esau" (Genesis 27:22).

On this basis Isaac proceeded to pronounce the blessing of the firstborn upon his second son. It was not by his hearing that Isaac was deceived, it was by his feeling. How many since have made shipwreck because they acted on their feelings, rather than on a definite word from the Lord. Faith does not build on feelings but on facts, on glorious certainties, and on a divine revelation that can never fail. We cannot exaggerate, therefore, the importance of having our ears attuned to every word that proceeds out of the mouth of God.

The Anointed Ear

In the day of his cleansing, the leper had sacrificial blood placed on the tip of his right ear, the thumb of his right hand, and the great toe of his right foot. After that the anointing oil was superimposed on the blood. (See Lev.14.) The blood-stained ear was an ear consecrated to hear God's word, and the superimposed oil, an emblem of the Holy Spirit, emphasised that the ultimate purpose of that consecration could only be realised in dependence upon the Spirit of God.

The same ceremony was performed on Aaron's sons when they were consecrated to the priesthood. As a matter of interest, on that occasion two significant things might be noted; (i) Aaron personally was first anointed, and (ii) Aaron's anointing took place before the blood of sacrifice was shed. In all this Aaron, the High Priest, points us to the uniqueness of the Lord Jesus Christ, hence a difference was made between Aaron and his sons.

When we apply the consecration of Aaron and his sons to this third song, the message seems to be that what was true of the Servant King in an absolute sense, can be true of us too, but only in a relative sense. Nevertheless it is our duty to cultivate both an anointed ear and a disciplined tongue as the disciples of the Lord Jesus. For in no other way will we be able to adorn the doctrine of God our Saviour.

First the Servant

It has always been an accepted principle of service among believing people, that the servant of the Lord must first be spoken to before he speaks. With a disciple's ear he will listen, and then, having learned his lesson well, he will speak God's word to others. His task is to communicate plainly what he has first of all received from the Lord. And this is how Isaiah envisaged the ministry of Messiah. He would take a disciple's place among His people in order to fulfil the role of a prophet. He will first hear God's words, and then He will declare them to His hearers.

The Lord Jesus often alluded to this principle in the course of His ministry. For instance, when He was in Jerusalem at the feast of Tabernacles. "The Jews marvelled, saying, How knows this man letters, having never learned? Jesus answered them, and said, My doctrine is not mine, but His that sent me" (John 7:15,16). And at a time of intense controversy with the Jewish leaders, He announced, "When you have lifted up the Son of Man, then shall you know that ... as the Father has taught me, I speak these things" (John 8:28).

To the disciples in the upper room, Jesus privately insisted, "The word that you hear is not mine, but the Father's, who sent me" (John14:24). And on another occasion He told them, "What I tell you in darkness, that speak in light; and what you hear in the ear, that proclaim upon the housetops" (Matt.10:27). Writing to the Corinthian church, Paul was able to claim, "I have received of the Lord that which also I delivered unto you" (1Cor.11:23). The prophet Haggai spoke of himself, and of his own prophetic ministry in the same way. "Then spoke Haggai, *the Lord's messenger*, in *the Lord's message* unto the people" (Hag.1:13).

The Covered Ear

Opened in the phrase "*the Lord God has opened my ear*" suggests, by implication, the idea of something that had been covered. It emphasises the importance of placing a guard by the eargate. In one place, our Lord said, "Take heed *what* you hear" (Mk.4:24), and in another, He said, "Take heed *how* you hear" (Luke 8:18). On the one hand, be cautious about what you hear; and then on the other, be discriminating in the use you make of what you have heard.

Talebearing

We must not lend our ears to every story that is doing the rounds, for defilement can so easily reach us through the eargate. The tongue is a little member, but when it is used to spread slander it can, and often does, occasion great mischief. One man's rule, when someone came to him with a story about a third party, was to ask three simple questions: (i) will it do the person any good about whom it is told? (ii) will it do any good to the person who is telling it? and (iii) will it do me any good to hear it? After that, the matter was usually dropped.

It is always mischievous to lend our ears to talebearing, for talebearing keeps stirring the pot. One of the prohibitions God placed upon His people in ancient times was this, "You shall not go up and down as a talebearer among your people." (See Lev.19:16.) We do well when we apply this pertinent scripture to ourselves, for "where there is no talebearer, the strife ceases" (Prov.26:20). The maintenance of a covered ear is a powerful preservative in these matters.

In his proverbs, King Solomon said, "Keep your heart with all diligence; for out of it are the issues of life" (Prov.4:23). Remove the first and last letters from 'heart' and you are left with the word 'ear'. There is an ear in every heart, and this is the ear our song refers to. We must secure it and cover it. Then, in the secret place, we must allow the Lord to lift the covering, and put His word into it. Such a word will enable us, in turn, to speak seasonably to weary souls.

Our Daily Bread

This was a daily occurrence with the perfect Servant, and it should be so with us as well. The children of Israel in the wilderness received the manna on a daily basis. Daily it was given, and daily it was gathered. And in what is often called the disciples' prayer, the Lord teaches us to pray and to say, "give us this day our daily bread."

There can be no doubt that our Saviour's public ministry was the fruit of a daily learning process in the secret place. The sharpened sword and the polished arrow of the previous song were plainly the result of long and careful preparation. How much more necessary it is for us to cultivate the anointed ear that listens daily to the voice of God.

We must make time to wait on the Lord so that He can speak to us through His word. In the process we shall find phrases, verses and passages that will stand out, and through them the Lord will speak directly into our hearts. A rewarding exercise is to write down those verses etc., and then to look at them throughout the day. In this way we will more easily commit them to memory, and store them in our hearts. In turn, they will become the very words we shall be able to speak to the help and blessing of others.

The Awakened Ear

The Servant also speaks of His ear being *awakened*. The word means to be alerted or called to attention. The idea it suggests is of applying our minds to the detail of any given matter. In reading the scriptures we tend to be too casual, we must be attentive to the fine print of what we read. Too often we are satisfied with vague generalisations in spiritual things; as a result, the real point is missed and the word of God becomes of no effect. We must cultivate the spirit of the Bereans, who searched the scriptures daily. Whatever they heard, even from an apostle, the Bereans had to have it verified from the scriptures. (See Acts17:11.)

Mary, the Lord's mother is a fine example of this very thing. She treasured the things she heard and "pondered them in her heart" (Luke 2:19). In the same way the word that God speaks into our hearts should be meditated upon and pondered, and actively applied to our various situations. But this will require us to take time over the scriptures, distinguishing between the various parts and comparing one scripture with another. (See 1Cor.2:13.)

A Morning Exercise

The best time to do this is in the morning, before the din of the new day begins, and before the clamour of other voices is heard. In the morning our minds are fresh, and we are more attentive to hear what the Lord might say to us for our guidance through the hours ahead. Our chief example in this, as in all things, is the Servant of Isaiah's songs. He could say, "*morning by morning; He wakens my ear to hear like the learned.*" This morning by morning exercise is not intended to be exceptional, it is to be the standard routine of all who claim discipleship in the school of Christ.

Wherever He was found, on board a fishing vessel with His disciples, or resting on a couch that had been prepared for Him by loving hands at Bethany, the Spirit touched Him early, and summoned Him to the lessons of the brand new day. One of the evangelists testified of Him, and said, "In the morning, rising up a great while before day, He went out, and departed into a solitary place, and there prayed" (Mark 1:35).

Before leaving this matter we might point out that some have linked the opened ear of the perfect Servant with the Hebrew servant whose ear was pierced with an awl at the doorpost of his master's house. (See Ex. 21.) Having served the years required by the law, he was now a free man. But instead of going out free, he assumed a place of perpetual service out of love for his master, and his wife and children. This decision was sealed by his ear being pierced at the door of the house. Thereafter, that woman and those children, could look upon that pierced ear, and read in it imperishable proof of that man's love for them.

We too, of course, can trace in every step of our suffering Saviour, powerful proofs of the love that found its highest expression in the cross. But strictly speaking, there is a difference between the two references. The pierced ear of the Hebrew servant points powerfully to the Lord Jesus who loved us even unto death, whereas the opened ear of Isaiah's Servant spells out the detailed and intelligent attention He gave to doing the Father's will throughout the entire course of His earthly pilgrimage.

The *Third Song*

The Afflictions of Messiah (Contd.)

I gave my back to the smiters (v.6)

Every student knows the importance of qualifications if he is to progress to further and higher education. And we know that there are basic and essential qualifications for entry into the school of God. We must have an attitude of subjection to His will, and of obedience to His word. In this respect the perfect Servant was eminently qualified, for He was able to say with complete sincerity, "*The Lord God has opened my ear, and I was not rebellious, neither turned away back*" (Isa.50:5).

The fuller meaning of this statement must be, that between the Lord and His Servant, there was perfect accord, there was no disagreement. To the Jews who gathered around Him in Solomon's porch at Jerusalem, Jesus was able to say, "I and my Father are one" (John10:30). Whatever else may have been involved in that claim, this much is clear, His will was one with the Father's will.

The Double Negative

The use of the double negative is simply another and stronger way of asserting His total abandonment to the will of God. It has been suggested that the first negative, *I was not rebellious* may indicate that there was no inward spirit of rebellion in Him; while the second, *neither turned away back* may mean that there was not even a hint of hesitancy on His part.

The gospel narratives tell of a constraint and an urgency that was ever pressing upon our Saviour during His earthly pilgrimage. At the age of twelve He said, "I must be about my Father's business" (Luke 2:49). On a certain occasion it was said of Him, "He must needs go through Samaria" (John 4:4). At about that same time He told the disciples, "My food is to do the will of Him who sent me, and to finish His work" (John 4:34). And yet again, "I have a baptism to be baptised with; and how am I straightened till it be accomplished" (Luke 12:50).

To speak of the Lord Jesus as if He had been weak or effeminate, lacking in real courage, and noted mainly for an attitude of passivity, would be an unwarranted caricature. All such suggestions are refuted by the resolve that moved Him to set His face like a flint and to tread the Calvary road. He did this with an awesome awareness of what lay ahead. The sorrows of Calvary were anticipated to the full in the garden where He prayed, "O my Father, if it be possible, let this cup pass from me." Quite clearly that cup represented something from which His soul would recoil. But then He added, "nevertheless, not as I will, but as thou wilt" (Matt.26:39).

The Rebellious Son

The subject Servant of our song stands in sharp contrast to the rebellious son, about whom we read in the Mosaic law. Parents whose son was stubborn and selfwilled, could bring charges against their boy, before the elders in the gate of the city where they lived. If the charges were sustained, the punishment was death by stoning. This was known as the law of the rebellious son. But there is no record, not even in a single instance, of that law having been invoked. (See Deut.21:18-21.)

Was ever a son more rebellious than David's son, Absalom? Yet in the hour of his untimely death, David lamented over him and said, "O my son Absalom, my son, my son Absalom! Would God I had died for thee, O Absalom, my son, my son" (2Sam.18:33). It seems never to have entered David's heart to invoke the ancient statute. Nor is the reason difficult to discover, for the instinct of every father's heart is to spare his son.

But when God's Son appeared in this world, the only son who could say with complete candour, *I was not rebellious*, we are told, "God spared not His own Son, but delivered Him up for us all" (Rom.8:32). What a startling contrast to David's attitude towards Absalom. The marvel of this is equalled only by the marvel of the Son's willingness to "*give His back to the smiters, and His cheeks to them that plucked off the hair*" (Isa.50:6).

If obedience and subjection, therefore, are essential qualifications for enrolment in God's school, they are not easy options. The likelihood is that they will carry unforeseen consequences, particularly in the realm of suffering and affliction. The perfect Servant, whose obedience put Him in marked contrast to the unresponsive nation to which He came, certainly found it so. Every would-be servant of Christ should ponder, deeply and often, what is recorded here of the perfect Servant's sufferings.

The Things He Suffered

It has been pointed out that all the forms of ill-treatment mentioned here, were traditional ways of dealing with criminals. Without hesitation we can say that they present an amazingly accurate statement of the sufferings of Christ. Here is a truly remarkable catalogue of events, written seven hundred years or more before they happened. It spells out in advance, and in great detail, the things the Lord of glory suffered at the hands of sinful men on the actual morning of the crucifixion.

Of course, the discerning mind will always differentiate between these sufferings and the atoning sufferings. The latter are the sufferings He endured when God laid upon Him the iniquity of us all. It is just not possible for us to follow Him in the things He suffered in order to make atonement for our souls. The winepress of Calvary He had to tread alone. Those vicarious or atoning sufferings are the principle subject of the final song.

In what is before us now we have a singular disclosure of the enmity of the natural heart towards the Lord from heaven. The natural man craves to do his own thing and to pursue his own desires. But the perfect Servant, treading a path of self-effacement and self-denial, was a rebuke to such proud pretensions. Inevitably, the humility and the abandonment to the will of God that marked the Lord Jesus would provoke a reaction, it would bring upon His head the wrath of sinful men.

The Servant's Obedience

Here then, we have distilled for us the very essence of true obedience. There is first an ear attuned to hear God speak, and alongside that, there is a spirit that is not rebellious. There is an absorbing desire to do the will of God whatever the cost. Of necessity this will involve a daily application of the cross to ourselves; it will mean having "the sentence of death in ourselves, that we should not trust in ourselves but in God, who raises the dead" (2Cor.1:9).

On the road to Golgotha, the Lord Jesus said to the daughters of Jerusalem, "If they do these things in a green tree, what shall be done in the dry" (Luke 23:31). The expression may have been no more than a familiar proverb of the time, but now it was spoken as a prophecy. Earlier Jesus had said to the disciples, "In the world you shall have tribulation: but be of good cheer; I have overcome the world" (John16:33). By these words, and many others, He sought to prepare His own for the afflictions that would assuredly come upon them.

The Suffering Church

Before long Stephen, the first Christian martyr, would be stoned, Paul would be beheaded and John would be exiled. But these were only earnests of the unspeakable atrocities that would be perpetrated, first by pagan Rome, and then by papal Rome, against the Lord's people across the centuries. When Marcus Aurelius came to the throne of the Caesars, in AD167, the profession of Christianity was declared a crime against the State. In those days, the wild beast, the axe, the cross, and the stake were the cruel forms of death meted out to faithful followers of our Lord Jesus Christ. (See Miller's Church History.)

Justin

Yet, the persecutions they endured had precisely the same effect on them as the indignities that were heaped on Christ had upon Him. They called forth striking and soul stirring protestations of faith. The saintly Justin who was born at Neapolis in Samaria, of Gentile parents, was one of the noblest characters in early Christian literature; he was cast into prison for his faith. Later he was scourged and finally beheaded. His dying testimony earned for him the surname 'Martyr', and to this day he is affectionately spoken of as Justin Martyr.

Polycarp

Polycarp of Smyrna was probably well past ninety years when he was arraigned before the Prefect. "Revile Christ and I will release thee," he said to the old man. Polycarp, with great dignity replied, "Six and eighty years have I served Him, and He has done me nothing but good; how could I revile Him, my Lord and Saviour?" Polycarp, like many others, reached the throne by way of the stake. All the trumpets must surely have sounded, loud and clear, on the other side.

These are only two of a great multitude of witnesses whose testimony was an echo of the resolve of the perfect Servant in this third song. In spite of the smiting, the shame and the spitting He boldly declared, "*The Lord God will help me ... therefore have I set my face like a flint, and I know that I shall not be ashamed*" (Isa.50:7). Such was "the faith of the Son of God" (Gal.2:20). Admittedly, our sufferings are on a different level from His, and yet the things that tested His faith will test ours as well.

And others also...

"And what shall we more say? For the time would fail us to tell of Gideon, and of Barak, and of Samson, and of Jephthah; of David also, and Samuel, and of the prophets, who, through faith, subdued kingdoms, obtained promises, stopped the mouths of lions, quenched the violence of fire, escaped the edge of the sword, out of weakness were made strong, became valiant in fight, turned to flight the armies of the aliens ... And others also ... " (Hebs.11:32-40).

The *Third Song*

The Help of God

The Lord God will help me (vv.7,9)

The human experience has ever been cast in the context of extremes; we may be happy and enjoying life, only to find ourselves in the next moment, confronted by death. But Paul said, "We are always confident" (2Cor.5:6). Godly confidence is not an idle boast, nor is it a blind refusal to recognise reality. It is a quiet assurance, born of the conviction that God is sovereign. That He is over all, and that He is working all things according to His own will.

Trust in the Sovereign Lord

Within the compass of three short verses, we find this extraordinary Servant of Isaiah's songs, affirming His confidence in God as His helper. First He says, "*For the Lord God will help me; therefore I shall not be confounded.*" Then He goes on to assert, "*He is near who justifies me. Who will contend with me*?" And finally He declares, "*Behold, the Lord God will help me, Who is he that shall condemn me? Lo, they all shall grow old as a garment; a moth shall eat them up*." (See Isa.50:7-9.)

"I will never leave thee, nor forsake thee," was an ancient pledge given by God to His people, and one that has held good in every age. In the epistle to the Hebrews, the writer recalls it, and adds his own response. Quoting some words from the Psalms, he wrote, "So we may boldly say, The Lord is my Helper, and I will not fear what man shall do unto me" (Hebs.13:5,6). The word *boldly* in this verse has nothing at all of arrogance about it. It is elsewhere rendered *confidently*.

These assertions of Isaiah's Servant, therefore, are more than just grit and doggedness. They are not to be interpreted as sheer defiance, for in the midst of all He endured, His hope was fixed in God. For our part, if we are to withstand the fiery darts of the wicked one, and the pressures of the age in which we live, nothing short of this will suffice. Only a living faith will enable us to remain true after the strain has passed.

O for a faith that will not shrink
Though pressed by many a foe.
That will not tremble on the brink
Of poverty or woe;

A faith that shines more bright and clear
When tempests rage without,
That when in danger knows no fear,
In darkness feels no doubt.

A Declared Faith

It is helpful to observe that this repeated affirmation of the Servant's faith served a double purpose. First, it had the effect of strengthening His own inner resolve (if we might so speak) to pursue the will of God to the utmost. Luke, the evangelist, reported, how at a certain point, "When the time was come that He should be received up, He steadfastly set His face to go to Jerusalem" (Luke 9:51). The point referred to was reached at the time of His transfiguration on the holy mount.

Leaving aside for a moment the overriding mediatorial purpose of His coming, which was to give His life a ransom for all, it would appear that from the holy mount He might have stepped back into heaven, and assumed again the place that was His from eternity. But instead of doing so, He came down from the mount and set His face as a flint, and willingly trod the Calvary road.

The other effect of His declared faith, was to emphasise the ultimate issue and the eventual triumph of His suffering and death. Every phrase in these verses is culled from the courtroom. They amplify our Lord's challenge to His accusers when they charged that He was possessed by a demon, "Which of you convinces me of sin?" (John 8:46) Here He throws down the gauntlet and says, "*Who then will bring charges against me? Let us face each other! Who is my accuser? Let him confront me*!" And again, "*Who is he that will condemn me*?" (Isa.50:8,9 *n.i.v.*)

But if not ...

A notable instance of this kind of faith was found in Daniel's three friends when they were about to be cast into the furness of fire, heated to seven times its normal heat. Standing before the greatest monarch this world has ever produced, the three men declared their faith. They said, "If it be so, our God, whom we serve, is able to deliver us from the burning fiery furness, and He will deliver us out of your hand, O king. *But if not*, be it known unto you, O king, that we will not serve your gods, nor worship the golden image which you have set up" (Dan.3:17,18). God honoured their faith in a dramatic and singular way; and they endured, as seeing Him who is invisible.

In the same way it is good for us to declare our faith, especially in times of adversity. "Let the redeemed of the Lord *say so*, whom He has redeemed from the hand of the enemy" (Psa.107:2). Ours is a '*say so*' faith. In confessing it we are inwardly strengthened, and as a result, God is glorified by an outworking of His grace in our lives. Even in those times when we cannot trace His *strange designs*, faith must still stand on His promises, and go on trusting.

For faith to be trusted, it has to be tested. Its endurance under testing will alone prove its reality. And true faith will always honour God, and dare to take Him at His word. Such a faith will embolden us, and borrowing another's words, it will enable us to say, "Why are you cast down, O my soul? And why are you disquieted within me? Hope in God; for I shall yet praise Him, who is the health of my countenance, and my God" (Psa.42:11).

The Servant Vindicated

Repeating His earlier conviction, "*The Lord God will help me,*" the Servant again proclaims His trust in the living God, the Sovereign Lord (v.9). This time He expresses it in two ways. In the first place He declares, "*He is near who justifies me.*" As the term is used here, justification is not to be understood in the theological sense of imputing righteousness to the sinner; rather it has the idea of vindication.

In an earlier song we touched on the vindication of Christ. We noted that scripture records the matter in a threefold way. The Lord Jesus was vindicated at His resurrection and subsequent exaltation. The fourth song begins at that precise point. It shows Him exalted, extolled and made very high. (See our comments on Isa.52:13.) When God raised the Lord Jesus from the dead, the integrity of every claim He had ever made was openly demonstrated.

There is a further vindication of Christ when sinners repent and believe the gospel. Referring to the ministry of the Holy Spirit, Jesus said, "When He is come, He will reprove [convince] the world of sin ... Of sin, because they believe not on me" (John16:8,9). In man's view sin has been so diluted, it is little more than a moral lapse or an infringement of commonly accepted traditions. But in God's view, sin is crystalised in the world's attitude to His Son: in the refusal of His creatures to believe on the Lord Jesus, that they might be saved. But multitudes have believed across the years, and in them we have a marvellous vindication of Christ, the only Saviour of men.

The ultimate vindication of the perfect Servant, however, will be seen at His coming again. In that day, God will set His Son upon His holy hill of Zion, and every eye shall behold Him enthroned in glorious majesty. (See Psa.2:6-9.) In this third song, the Servant expresses His confidence in that ultimate vindication in the way He speaks of those who became His enemies wrongfully. "*They all shall grow old like a garment; the moth shall eat them up*" (Isa.50:9).

These are plainly images of inevitable destruction. If the Servant's confidence found its first answer in His resurrection, it certainly looked forward to His return as well and to the glory of His second advent.

Who is among you that fears the Lord?

The last two verses of our chapter have been the subject of much debate. Do they form a part of the song, or are they simply a comment on it? Is the speaker in these verses the Father or the Servant?

v.11. "Who is among you that fears the Lord, that obeys the voice of His servant, that walks in darkness, and has no light? Let him trust in the name of the Lord, and stay upon his God.

v.12. Behold, all you that kindle a fire, that compass yourselves about with sparks: walk in the light of your fire, and in the sparks that you have kindled. This shall you have of my hand; you shall lie down in sorrow."

Probably, it is best to think of both verses as summarising the essential thrust of the song. But having said that, how should we understand them? The majority of expositors seem to favour the idea that the verses refer to the two generations that can be traced through the scriptures from the very beginning.

The first verse they identify with the generation of faith, which was personalised in Abel; and the second verse, the generation of unbelief, personalised in Cain. The former, trusting in the living God, and yet seeming to find trouble at every turn. The latter, while appearing to see everything clearly, in the end can only lie down in sorrow. This view of life is helpfully amplified in Psalm 73, a Psalm that, in any case, should be required and regular reading for every believer.

There is another view, however, which might be even more pertinent. Solomon said, "Trust in the Lord with all your heart, and lean not unto your own understanding" (Prov.3:5). The inclination of the spiritual man is always to fear the Lord and to obey His voice, even when he treads an uncertain path. When the clouds seem to be closing in, he still trusts in the name of the Lord, believing that 'it is better to walk with God in the dark, than to go alone in the light.'

On the other hand, the carnally minded man inclines to his own understanding. He kindles his own fire, and he walks in the light of the sparks that come from it. He will lay aside the commandments of God, and hold to the traditions of men instead. (See Mark 7:8.) For a time he can rejoice in a way that seems right, but inevitably, the end of that way is death.

Perhaps Paul had these very things in mind when he wrote, "For to be carnally minded is death, but to be spiritually minded is life and peace" (Rom.8:6). The scriptures abound with illustrations of this principle, but the perfect Servant of Jehovah is the consummate example of Solomon's instruction to trust in the Lord. And our happiness is assured as we follow in His steps.

Whatever our understanding of these concluding verses may be, they certainly challenge us to respond to the perfect Servant by making Him the pattern and model of our lives. When we find ourselves in circumstances where no light can be seen, our hearts are cheered as we remember Him. To every believer, beset by fightings without, or fears within, the exhortation is plain, "let him trust in the name of the Lord, and stay upon his God" (Isa.50:10). The united response of a great cloud of witnesses in every age is that 'they who trust Him wholly, find Him wholly true.'

Stayed upon Jehovah,
Hearts are fully blest;
Finding, as He promised,
Perfect peace and rest.

The God of Recovery

We cannot close our study of the third song without referring back to the two most interesting questions with which it began. We have already considered them and learned their significance. From a spiritual point of view, Israel today is in the position of a divorced wife, and of a slave who has sold herself into the service of an enemy.

But neither of these positions is irretrievable, and in the end, a mighty recovery will take place that will parallel Israel's original redemption from Egypt. This highlights a very special and important factor; the God whom we serve is a God of recovery, a God of revival and of restoration. "Behold, I am the Lord, the God of all flesh, is there anything too hard for me" (Jer.32:27).

The History of Revival

(i) In Israel

The element of revival, of recovery and restoration, can be traced throughout Israel's long and eventful history. After the death of Joshua, and of the elders who outlived Joshua, the people lapsed into appalling apostasy. As a result they found themselves subjected to the cruel rule of the king of Mesopotamia. But when they humbled themselves and repented, God raised up a deliverer, a man called Othniel, who delivered them from their bondage and restored the situation.

Following the death of Othniel, the people again turned away from the Lord and once more they were brought into servitude, this time to the king of Moab. After some time, and again upon their repentance, the Lord raised up Ehud, and once more the situation was restored. Later they came under the power of the Philistines. But when they repented and turned to the Lord, Shamgar became their judge and they found another wonderful deliverance.

Later still, the Canaanites subdued them, but God raised up Deborah. And when the Midianites came and destroyed their crops, they cried again unto the Lord, and He heard their cry. He gave them Gideon, and with him He gave them victory over their foes. In the behalf of His people, the Lord showed Himself, time and again, to be a God of recovery. This is the message of the entire period covered by the book of Judges.

(ii) In the Church

The history of the Church tells the same tale. It is the story of a series of departures from the Lord, and of numerous declensions, followed by gracious revivings. We can read the history of the 17th century in America, and of the great revival that took place there, mainly through the ministry of Jonathan Edwards. A similar happening occurred in England in the 18th century under the ministries of George Whitfield and of John and Charles Wesley. Later there was the well documented Ulster revival in the middle of the 19th century. And in the 20th century, there were widely reported seasons of revival in Wales and in Scotland.

Of course, the greatest revival in history was when the exiles of the first dispersion returned from Babylon. But even that, and all the revivals we have called attention to, will pale into insignificance in comparison with what will take place, when the Lord turns His hand the second time to recover the remnant of His people Israel. In that day, He will bring His exiles from the four corners of the earth.

The Hope of Revival

For our part, we cherish both a primary and a secondary hope. The primary hope is "the coming of the Lord and our gathering together unto Him" (2Thess.2:1). That hope is pledged; it will take place when God's time comes. But while it tarries, we cherish a secondary hope. It is the hope of revival. This is not pledged; it is in the sovereign gift of God, and there are conditions attached to it. We must humble ourselves, as Israel did in the period of the Judges. We must give ourselves afresh to the Lord, and pray that the God of recovery might grant to us a reviving, even as we wait for His Son from heaven.

Revive Your work, O Lord!
Your mighty arm make bare;
Speak with the voice that wakes the dead,
And make Your people hear.

13 Behold, my servant shall deal prudently; he shall be exalted and extolled, and be very high.
14 As many were astounded at thee; his visage was so marred more than any man, and his form more than the sons of men:
15 So shall he sprinkle many nations; the kings shall shut their mouths at him; for that which had not been told them shall they see, and that which they had not heard shall they consider.
1 Who hath believed our report of the Lord revealed?
2 For he shall grow up before him like a tender plant, and like a root out of a dry ground; he hath no form nor comeliness, and when we shall see him, there is no beauty that we should desire him.
3 He is despised and rejected of men, a man of sorrows, and acquainted with grief, and we hid as it were our faces from him; he was despised, and we esteemed him not.
4 Surely he hath borne our griefs, and carried our sorrows; yet we did esteem him stricken, smitten of God, and afflicted.
5 But he was wounded for our transgressions, he was bruised for our iniquities; the chastisement [for] our peace was upon him, and with his stripes we are healed.
6 All we like sheep have gone astray; we have turned every one to his own way, and the Lord hath laid on him the iniquity of us all.
7 He was oppressed, and he was afflicted, yet he opened not his mouth; he is brought as a lamb to the slaughter, and as a sheep before her shearers is dumb, so he openeth not his mouth.? And to whom is the arm
8 He was taken from prison and from judgement; and who shall declare his generation? For he was cut off out of the land of the living; for the transgression of my people was he stricken.
9 And he made his grave with the wicked, and with the rich in his death, because he had done no violence, neither was any deceit in his mouth.
10 Yet it pleased the Lord to bruise him; he hath put him to grief. When thou shalt make his soul an offering for sin, he shall see his seed, he shall prolong his days, and the pleasure of the Lord shall prosper in his hand.
11 He shall see of the travail of his soul, and shall be satisfied; by his knowledge shall my righteous servant justify many; for he shall bear their iniquities.

12 Therefore will I divide him a portion with the great, and he shall divide the spoil with the strong, because he hath poured out his soul unto death; and he was numbered with the transgressors; and he bore the sin of many, and made intercession for the transgressors.

4th Servant Song: Isa. 52:13 - Isa. 53:12

The *Fourth Song*

The Servant's Triumph

The fifteen verses of this song form a pentateuch. They divide into five equal parts, with three verses in each part. In this, they are like the book of Psalms which also divides into five parts. Other pentateuchs are formed by the five books of Moses at the beginning of the Old Testament, and also by the first five books in the New Testament. Taken together the four Gospels and the Acts of the Apostles combine to make up the New Testament's historical section.

There are other similar divisions in scripture, but none is more profound than what we have here in the five stanzas of this fourth song. It will come as no surprise to be told that this is the Old Testament passage most frequently quoted in the New Testament. Moreover, the impressive and very extensive writings, both Jewish and Christian, ancient and modern, that are based on this passage simply confirm its interest and its importance.

This final song is freely acknowledged to be the superlative Old Testament passage on Messiah's sufferings. For this reason, the focus of the reader's attention tends to be on those sufferings. But while this may be so, we should always keep before us, that the song looks beyond the sufferings, to the glory still to be revealed. It begins with Messiah's present exaltation, and ends with His future glory. And since these are the parameters within which the whole is presented, it follows that the future glory of Christ has to be one of the song's significant features.

In an earlier chapter we noted that when the Hebrew prophets looked forward to the coming of Christ, they sometimes had difficulty harmonising the two advents. But there can be no question that both advents are profoundly intertwined in this fourth song. Here we are able to reflect on the depths of Messiah's humiliation and to ponder the heights of His exaltation. This fourth song allows us to look back upon the sufferings of the first advent, while at the same time enabling us to anticipate the glories of the second.

The Way of the Cross

Most readers simply apply this song to themselves, and well they might, for there are great truths here which have to be of universal application. Having said that, it should be recognised that there are also features in this song that bear directly on Israel, both in the past, and in the future. This important detail was acknowledged by Caiaphas who was High Priest in the year of our Lord's crucifixion. "He prophesied that Jesus should die for that nation; and not for that nation only, but that also He should gather together in one the children of God that were scattered abroad" (John11:51,52).

Moreover, the references to nations and to kings at the beginning of the song, seem to indicate that it has a relevance to the Gentile nations as well. Those very nations that were so much before us in the earlier songs are again brought to our attention. "So shall He sprinkle many nations; kings shall shut their mouths at Him … " (Isa.52:15). The transcendent message of the fourth song, therefore, seems to be that the cross of Christ is the single ground of God's dealings with all men, whether in the past, the present or the future.

Throughout the Old Testament period individuals were saved by grace and through faith. (See Hebs.11.) In this age the Lord Jesus is said to be *the Saviour of the body* [the Church]. And we are told that in a coming day, *all Israel will be saved* (Rom.11:26). In addition, we read of *the nations of them who are saved*, and who will take their place in the future kingdom (Rev.21:24). But no one has ever been saved, or ever will be saved, apart from the blood of the cross. All the things predicted in the servant songs will be accomplished only by virtue of the cross.

Admittedly these are preliminary and background considerations, but they do impress upon us the tremendous scope of this final song. They will also serve, as guidelines, to lead us into the profound truths that are here spread before us. This final song begins properly at chapter 52:13, and concludes at chapter 53:12.

In the chapter that follows (Ch.54) we have a further call to sing praise: "Sing, O barren ... break forth into singing ... says the Lord" (Isa.54:1). Having noted that this call to praise is a feature common to all the songs we are using it here again, as we have done in the other songs, as the marker which brings this final song to a close.

The *Fourth Song*

Stanza No. 1

My servant shall deal prudently

The final song begins like the first, with a call to "*Behold, my Servant.*" In this way the Holy Spirit follows the now familiar pattern. He sets forth the divine intention for the Servant and then proceeds to show how that end will be attained. "*Behold, my Servant shall deal prudently; He shall be exalted and extolled, and be very high*" (Isa.52:13).

His Exaltation

The expression, "My servant shall *deal prudently*" might be rendered My servant shall *act wisely*. Isaiah had earlier declared, "the Spirit of the Lord shall rest upon Him, the spirit of wisdom and understanding, the spirit of counsel ... etc. (Isa.11:2). Since He was led by the Spirit, the Lord Jesus was always governed by the wisdom that is from above, and not by the wisdom of this world which is of wholly different order.

The apostle James urged his readers to guard against the false wisdom. He defined the wisdom that descends not from above as being earthly, sensual and devilish. Noting the nature of heavenly wisdom, He said, "The wisdom that is from above is first pure, then peaceable, gentle, and easy to be entreated, full of mercy and good fruits, without partiality, and without hypocrisy" (James 3:17).

These gracious features were ever present in the life of our wonderful Lord. Like flowers in a well appointed garden, they grew and blossomed in beautiful harmony. Grace and truth were always in perfect balance in His flawless life. And when that life was laid down in death, the Father was so completely glorified, He raised the Lord Jesus from the dead and gave Him glory.

In one sense, scripture views the exaltation of the Lord Jesus as a reward for His self-humbling. It was because He humbled Himself, that He has now been highly exalted. (See Phil.2:8,9.) Here in the beginning of this fourth song, and as a consequence of His prior obedience unto death, we find Him *exalted* and *extolled*, and made *very high.*

The terms employed are usually taken to signify degrees in the glorification of Christ. *Exalted* might be translated *raised up* and may refer to His resurrection. His ascension into heaven might answer to His being *extolled.* And being *made very high* probably has in view the risen and ascended Christ taking His place at God's right hand. Or it may even be, that being *made very high* identifies God's intention for His Son, while the other terms simply show how that purpose would be achieved.

His Humiliation

The Marred Visage

Because the path to the throne was the way of the cross we now read, "*As many were astounded at thee; His visage was so marred more than any man, and His form more than the sons of men*" (v.14). This somewhat evocative language is usually understood as referring to a facial disfiguration, sustained by our Lord, as a result of the physical sufferings inflicted on Him.

If this be so, it is quite remarkable that in the resurrection records there is not even a single mention of His face. We read of His hands, of His feet and of His side, but not of His face. Yet if this verse speaks of something purely physical, it must surely have had some implications for the resurrection morning which was only three days later.

On this matter we must speak with becoming reserve for we are treading on holy ground. It is true that the cross was heavy, but then, hundreds of people had carried the cross. The nails were sharp, but the same was true for the thieves who were crucified with Him. We dare not, and we will not, minimize the physical things our Saviour suffered at the hands of wicked men, nor will we detract from the pain He had to bear. But we must consider that these words may look beyond the purely physical and carry a deeper and fuller significance.

At one time or another, we have all met people who were suffering intense physical or emotional pain. They could feel the pain although they could not see it; for our part, we did not feel the pain but we certainly saw it. We saw it in their facial expressions and in their severely contorted countenances. It may be that this is the sense in which we should think of the marred visage.

When all that human malice could conceive had been done to His dear Son, God stepped in and did what God alone could do. He made the death of the Lord Jesus a sacrifice for sin. "He laid on Him the iniquity of us all" (Isa.53:6). Under that incalculable load of human sin and the awful stroke of the unrestrained wrath of God, His human form was so writhed in anguish, and His face so contorted, that all who beheld stared at Him in disbelief. They placed their hands over their mouths in stunned silence, and gaped upon Him in astonishment. That tender face had become so stricken in grief, it had the appearance of being scarcely human.

The Ruin of Tyre

The term Isaiah used is also used to describe the astonishment felt by those who saw the ruined city of Tyre. (See Ez.27:35.) Tyre, a seaport on the eastern shore of the Mediterranean Sea just north of Accho, was once the commercial capital of the ancient world. But when both the city and its king, gave themselves over to Satan, they came under the judgement of God, and both were destroyed. Tyre stood in relation to Jerusalem in much the same way as Babylon will stand in relation to the New Jerusalem in the last days. The lamantation at the fall of Babylon, therefore, will have its historical

parallel in the awful wailing over the fallen city of Tyre. (See Rev.18;9-24.)
Just as men stood stupified before the devastated city, so those who witnessed the Lord's humiliation upon the cross, among them the three Marys and John, the beloved disciple, stood spellbound at the horrific spectacle that met their gaze. "Behold, and see if there be any sorrow like unto my sorrow, which is done unto me, with which the Lord has afflicted me in the day of His fierce anger" (Lam.1:12). Of course, we are out of our depth when we attempt to define the sufferings of Christ, for here are waters to swim in.

What He endured, no tongue can tell,
To save our souls from death and hell.

His Manifestation in Glory

At this point the prophet points us forward to the glory of Christ and shows us that the depth of the degradation to which He was subjected will have its complete and unambiguous answer in the splendour in which He will yet be revealed. ***As** many were astounded* ... v14, ***so** shall He astound many* ... v.15.

Although Paul makes an application of this to the preaching of the gospel in this age (Rom.15:21), there can be no doubt that the passage anticipates the Servant's future advent when "every eye shall see Him, and they also who pierced Him; and all kindreds of the earth shall wail because of Him" (Rev.1:7).

We know that Peter, James and John were "eye-witnesses of His majesty" when they were with Him on the mount of transfiguration. Mark, who probably recorded much of what Peter had told him, says that when Jesus was transfigured before the three apostles, His "raiment became shining, exceedingly white like snow, as no fuller on earth can whiten them" (Mark 9:3).

Paul, too, spoke of the second advent in terms of "the brightness of His coming" (2Thess.2:8). He probably had a foreview of this on the Damascus Road, when he saw a light above the brightness of the noonday sun. But those experiences on the Holy Mount, and on the

Damascus Road, were only momentary flashes of the glory that is yet to be revealed.

The Lord Jesus, presently exalted at God's right hand, and seated with the Father, on the Father's throne, has been given a Name that is above every name. But when He comes again in the dazzling splendour of His second advent, every knee will bow before Him and kings will shut their mouths at Him, they will gape on Him in silent amazement. They will bring their glory and honour to His feet, and acknowledge Him to be the King above all kings. And in that day the nations will finally own His sway.

And the beauty of the Saviour will dazzle every eye,
In the crowning day that's coming, bye and bye.

The *Fourth Song*

Stanza No. 2

Who has believed our report ...?

Part two of this wonderful pentateuch begins with two related questions. "Who has believed our report, and to whom is the arm of the Lord revealed?" (Isa. 53:1) *Our report* is the report we have received, the report that has been brought to us, rather than a report given by us.

Whatever the range of their application, the primary interpretation of these questions must be to the elect nation to whom had been given the oracles of God. Israel had heard God speaking, time and again, through the prophets, the last of whom was John the Baptist. Finally, God sent unto them His only Son. "Last of all, He sent unto them His Son, saying, They will reverence my Son" (Matt.21:37).

The second question is also full of meaning. "*The arm of the Lord*" should not to be understood as referring to a limb, such as a forearm, or even to some kind of agency, something apart or separate from the Lord Himself. The term is used symbolically to denote the power of God exercised on the behalf of His people. (See Ex.15:16.) It denotes the Lord's very presence, personally and powerfully revealed.

If the question is asked, to whom did the Lord Jesus reveal Himself in the first instance? The answer can only be, to the house of Israel. Several times He stated with emphasis His prior mission to Israel.

He declared, for instance, "I am not sent but to the lost sheep of the house of Israel" (Matt.15:24). The historical record is clear and unambiguous, it says, "He came unto His own, but His own received Him not" (John 1:11).

Messiah's Rejection

In the first twelve chapters of John's gospel the Lord's public ministry was directed primarily to the elect people. Besides the witness of His words; which is most pronounced in chapters five to eight, there was the witness of His works. John recorded seven mighty miracles, all of them serving as specific signs to the house of Israel. Beginning at the marriage in Cana, where He turned water into wine, and ending at Bethany where He raised Lazarus from the dead.

We must emphasise that those mighty works were more than just miracles, they were definite and meaningful signs, performed in the presence of all the people. They substantiated the witness of His words and accredited all His claims. But in the end it had become woefully clear that the nation simply would not recognise her Messiah.

Recording these events, John, the evangelist, summed matters up like this: "Though He had done so many miracles among them, yet they believed not on Him" (John 12:42). It is also of interest to note that John linked this rejection of Christ with Isaiah's prediction of the consequent blindness that would befall the nation.

It is, therefore, in the Lord Jesus we have the answer to these questions, "*Who has believed our report, and to whom is the arm of the Lord revealed*?" Having heard Messiah's gracious words and having seen His mighty works, Israel still cried out, "We will not have this man to reign over us."

The Rationale

By what rationale did the nation treat Him thus? Why was He despised and rejected and why was all this done in a manner so dismissive? We addressed these questions at some length in the previous song. But the heart of the matter is suggested by the central verse of this second stanza. "*For He shall grow up before Him as a tender plant, and as a root out of a dry ground: He has no form nor comeliness: and when we shall see Him, there is no beauty that we should desire Him*" (Isa.53:2).

The Years of Obscurity

Princes usually grow up in public view and are allowed to cultivate a public image. From their earliest days they are trained to conduct themselves in the presence of people from every strata of society. They are groomed in the art of handling emergencies and of reacting to changing situations. They are presented to their public in circumstances of distinction, and in contexts of pomp and pageantry.

But this was not true of the one who now presented Himself to Israel. He was David's heir, and their Messiah, and yet He grew up at Nazareth and not in the capital city. Moreover, He had been born in a stable and not in a palace. It is true that Israel had been forewarned that her light would rise in obscurity (Isa.58:10), but when the time came, those very circumstances proved an occasion of stumbling. The people had been looking for a Goliath, and God had sent them a David. And while at the first they simply failed to recognise Him, in the end, they stubbornly refused to do so.

The Silent Years

Our Saviour's earthly life was in two quite distinct periods, the first thirty years, usually referred to as the years of obscurity; and the remaining three and a half years, the years of His public ministry. The first part is before us in the words, "*He shall grow up **before Him** as a tender plant.*" However interesting it might be to know more about the Lord Jesus during those early silent years, they are hidden from our view. For thirty years, from the time of His birth until the inauguration of His public ministry, scripture records only one brief mention of the Lord Jesus.

Enough is revealed, however, to let us know that He grew up, a subject child, in a home where the word of God was revered. He worked at the carpenter's bench alongside Joseph who, it would seem, died while Jesus was still a young man. We might therefore reasonably infer that, while still quite young, He was required to assume the place of the head of the family and shoulder responsibility for His now widowed mother, and for His brothers and sisters who were all His juniors.

But although out of public view, those years were spent under the eye of God. The ear of Jesus was always open to the voice of His Father in heaven. The sacred scriptures were ever His joy and delight, and at the age of twelve He formally took His place as a true Israelite. The one who had come to fulfil the types and shadows of the ceremonial law had at last appeared on the scene. Presently, the time would come for Him to assume a public role.

But it was not until His baptism, at the age of thirty, that the Father's voice was heard for the first time, publicly acknowledging His Son. He declared, "This is my beloved Son in whom I am well pleased" (Luke 3:22). Without doubt this familiar statement summed up the Father's delight in the Son's life during the waiting years at Nazareth.

The Public Ministry

There followed the three and a half years of His public ministry, during which He was subjected to the most intense and detailed scrutiny. After that the nation gave its verdict. It had been pre-announced by Isaiah in these words, "*He has no form nor comeliness and when we looked upon Him there was no beauty that we should desire Him.*" The word used for *comeliness* is also translated *majesty.* (See Psa.21:5.) It conveys the idea of regal splendour and royal pretension, the absence of which was such a feature of our Lord's earthly pilgrimage.

It could be implied from the nation's verdict that our Lord was not in any marked way, physically attractive. He may not have had a noticably beautiful appearance. They said, *There was no beauty that we should desire Him.* In any case, He certainly did not exude an aura of ostentation or regal splendour, nor did He move in a circle marked by all the sophistication of the capital city. Nazareth, where He had been brought up, had actually become a byword among the people, and so they blandly dismissed Him with the remark, "Can any good thing come out of Nazareth?"

Nor did the Lord Jesus move among the ruling classes, His companions were not the great ones of the earth. At His birth He was cradled in a manger and during the public years His everyday life was simplicity itself. It was summed up like this, "The foxes have holes, and the birds of the air have nests, but the Son of man has no where to lay His head" (Matt.8:20). In every particular He presented Himself to the nation in lowly guise.

Paul taught the Corinthians to distinguish between the treasure they had in Christ, and the vessel in which they possessed it. "We have this treasure in earthen vessels, that the excellency of the power might be of God, and not of us" (2Cor.4:7). Pre-occupation with the vessel tends to obscure the treasure it contains. As the old proverb so rightly says, *never judge the book by its cover.*

Much thought for the body and none for the soul is a fairly general truism in today's society. Yet the soul is the treasure while the body is really only the outer shell. The people of Israel rejected their promised Messiah because they judged the Lord by feeble sense, and saw Him only in terms of the earthen vessel. They failed to see in that human form, the presence of the Lord of glory. This understanding of the text seems to be confirmed by the fact that at this point Isaiah introduces two familiar horticultural metaphors, *a tender plant* and *a root out of a dry ground.*

A little boy thought his mother's hands so ugly because they were covered by the scars of severe burning. Then one day she explained that, before he could even remember, he had almost perished in a terrible fire but those very hands had plucked him from the jaws of death and in doing so had suffered so much. From that time forward, those hands that had seemed so ugly, now seemed the most beautiful hands in the world.

There was a time when we too could see no beauty in Christ, but then our eyes were opened by the Spirit of God to see Him in an altogether new and living way. We saw Him as our sin-bearer and as our substitute. We saw the suffering Servant as having suffered for us. We saw the crown of thorns as the symbol of the curse He bore for us. In His triumphant cry, "It is finished," we heard an echo of the satisfaction that will forever maintain us as justified sinners in the presence of God.

Of course the change was in us, and not in Him. But what a change! It was a regeneration, a new birth. The experience revolutionised our thinking about Christ, and from that time He has become the fairest of all the earth beside, and the chiefest among ten thousand to our souls. And such is the constraint of His love, we are ready to declare,

Naught that I have, my own I'll call,
I'll hold it for the giver.
My Lord , my life, my way, my all;
Are His, And His forever.

(a) What He Suffered *from* Men

The Nation's response

But Isaiah presses the charge against the nation still further. It was not simply that our Lord was rejected, He was actually despised. "*He is despised and rejected of men*" (v.3), These two words represent cause and effect. His rejection by His own people was so complete it can easily be traced from the very beginning of His public ministry to its end.

Think first of what happened at Nazareth when He publicly read from their own scriptures. He claimed that those very scriptures were being fulfilled before their eyes, and His listeners marvelled at the gracious words that proceeded out of His mouth. But that same day, no doubt urged on by their leaders, those same people, "thrust Him out of the city, and led Him unto the brow of the hill on which their city was built, that they might cast Him down headlong. But He, passing through the midst of them, went His way" (Luke 4:29,30).

Later, He came to Gadara where one of His most notable miracles was performed. The demons exorcised from the unfortunate man who dwelt among the tombs, entered into a herd of swine which then ran down a steep place and was drowned in the sea. But when the owners of the swine came from the city to see for themselves, they besought the Saviour to depart from them. Their only concern was for their swine, they had no regard for the Christ. Nor was that the last time property was placed above the welfare of people.

So far as Jesus was concerned it seemed that nobody would have Him, and the reality of this unpleasant fact was ultimately revealed in the judgement hall. Pilate at the first declared His innocence, and then vacillated, and finally, when he would have released Him, he succumbed to people power and did an about turn and delivered Him to be crucified. The people had spoken, they had demanded that Jesus should die. As at His birth there was no room for Him in the inn, so in the end, the only place that could be found for Him was the place called Calvary.

He was despised

But why should He have attracted such outright rebuttal? After all, He went about doing good and healing all that were oppressed of the Devil. He had shown Himself to be the greatest benefactor their nation had ever seen. The answer to our question lies in the phrase, "*He was despised*." As though to call attention to it, this word *despised* is used twice in a single verse. What does it signify?

The same word is rendered *vile* in the fifteenth Psalm. Discussing the things that are offensive to the godly man, the Psalmist said, "In whose eyes a *vile* person is contemned [contemptible]" (Psa.15:4). It is likely that Isaiah deliberately chose this term to express the attitude of men's hearts to the only begotten Son of God. The word certainly had a vivid historical connotation for the Jews at the time of Jesus, and this probably impacted very deeply upon their thinking. Daniel, the prophet, had predicted the rising up of a vile person who would come in peaceably and would seek to obtain the kingdom by flatteries ... (Dan.11:21).

Antiochus Epiphanes

Daniel's prophecy was fulfilled in Antiochus Epiphanes whose name stands second to none in infamy in the long chronicle of Hebrew history. Expositors frequently speak of him as the Antichrist of the Old Testament. He was personally so degraded that his lack of discipline and his carousals earned him the nickname 'Epimanes' which means *madman* in place of his assumed title 'Epiphanes' which means *illustrious*.

Such was his antagonism to the Jewish people, no atrocity either against them or against their religion, was too great for him to perpetrate. He was so violently anti-Semitic that with the aid of certain traitorous Jews he had a statute of Jupiter set up in the temple at Jerusalem. He went even further and superimposed a pagan altar on the the altar of burnt offering, and then, he commited the ultimate abomination, for he ordered that a pig, an unclean animal, should be sacrificed on that altar.

The word Isaiah used was carefully chosen. It forcefully conveys the nation's attitude to her Messiah, since it would almost certainly have conjured up in the Jewish mind images of Antiochus. For Jesus to be identified with a figure in history of such contempt, made it virtually certain that his own would not receive Him. And such was their disdain that, when the time came, they chose a murderer and rejected their own Messiah. They passed Him by and turned away their faces from Him.

Israel - Past and Future

It is most interesting to note that the closing part of this verse is recorded in the past tense. "And *we hid* as it were our faces from Him; *He was despised*, and *we esteemed* Him not" (v.3). Is it possible that in these precise words, restored Israel in a future day will confess the sins of unbelieving Israel in that former day?

The phrase, *we esteemed Him not*, suggests the idea that they could not bring themselves to impute a single honourable motive to our Saviour. When He healed a man who had a withered hand, they charged Him with being a sabbath-breaker. When He cast out demons, they said He was in league with Satan and that He cast out devils by Beelzebub, the prince of the devils. (See Matt.12.) No matter what He did they could not find one good word to say about Him. Although the common people heard Him gladly, the attitude of their leaders, with one or two exceptions, was always negative.

It is inconceivable that the Lord Jesus whose soul was sensitive beyond our comprehension, would have been impervious to the multiplied wounds He sustained in the house of His friends. Indeed, what is here recorded enables us to understand in some small way what moved Him to say, as we read in the second song, "I have laboured in vain, I have spent my strength for nothing, and in vain" (Isa.49:4).

In this stanza He is described as a *man of sorrows and acquainted with grief.* But He had not been born a man of sorrows, this is rather what He became as the result of being despised and rejected. He was acquainted with grief to such a degree that eventually He cried out in the words of a great messianic psalm, "Reproach has broken my heart" (Psa.69:21). So personally identified was He with sorrow and grief, He was given the name *a man of sorrows.*

Man of sorrows' what a name,
For the Son of God ...

Some will want to discuss the immediate physical cause of the Saviour's death. But here we must tread with caution for He said, "I lay down my life ... I have power to lay it down, and I have power to take it again" (John10:17,18). And yet, perhaps the Psalmist does give some insight into the matter in the words already quoted, "Reproach has broken my heart." At any rate the hymn-writer, with much feeling, picked up this idea and wrote,

He died of a broken heart for me,
He died of a broken heart.
O wondrous love, how great, how free,
He died of a broken heart.

Stanza No. 3

Surely He has borne our griefs

Stanza number three of this extraordinary pentateuch has its parallel in the third book of Moses, the book of Leviticus. Here we find ourselves in the inner sanctuary, in the Holy of Holies. At this point the twin truths of sin and substitution are introduced for the first time in the song, and the vicarious nature of Christ's death is emphasised. Our sins were the occasion of His sufferings, and it is *by His stripes we are healed.*

In discusssing the sufferings of Christ it might be helpful for us to think of them along three lines. Having considered just now what He suffered *from* men, we must pause to consider what He suffered *with* men during the course of His earthly sojourn. And only then shall we go on to think about what He suffered *for* men.

(b) What He Suffered *with* Men

There must be a reason for His rejection beyond what appears on the surface, and beyond anything that we have advanced so far. The opening word *Surely, "Surely He has borne our griefs ...* "v.4. carries the idea of explanation. Whatever people might have said, or thought, of His sufferings, the reality is this. There then follows a series of emphatic pronouns, "*He [Himself)] bore our [our very own] griefs and carried our [our very own] sorrows.*"

Matthew applies these words to our Lord's healing ministry, but evidently that did not completely exhaust their meaning. (See Matt.8:17.) Grief and sorrow are the consequence of sin, and who can measure the weight of grief and sorrow that plagues the human breast. The Lord Jesus was always aware of the sufferings of the multitudes who pressed upon Him from every side during the course of His ministry.

Many times we are told how He was moved with compassion. "When He saw the multitudes, He was moved with compassion on them, because they were faint, and were scattered abroad, as sheep having no shepherd" (Matt.9:36). Far from being impervious to human suffering, He was personally and emotionally involved with the people to whom He ministered. On one occasion, after performing a notable miracle of healing, we are told that virtue went out of Him. (See Luke 8:46.) It could truly be said that in all their afflictions, He was afflicted.

But it was too much to expect that the leaders of the people would understand what was taking place before their eyes. They persuaded themselves that what He endured was the just judgement of God and they concluded that it was all because of His own sins. From this conclusion, they rationalised their rejection of the One whom God had sent.

They argued that His affliction *must* be the judgement of God, since, in their view, He had been guilty of two capital offences; (i) sabbath breaking, and (ii) blasphemy. The report of the fourth evangelist stated, "the Jews therefore sought the more to kill Him, because He not only had broken the sabbath, but said also that God was His Father, making Himself equal with God" (John 5:18). We believe and are sure that His claim's were true, and we know that Israel too will accept that this is so in a coming day.

The pronoun *we* in the second part of this verse, as in an earlier verse, suggests that this song is probably the confession, written in advance, of the restored remnant at the time of the second advent. Israel in that future day will confess the sins of Israel in those former days in these precise terms, "*yet we did esteem Him stricken, smitten of God and afflicted.*"

(c) What He Suffered *for* Men

It is important to note how verse five begins, "*But He was wounded ...*" This marks a contrast with what has gone before. The sufferings now described are of a different character from all His other sufferings. Here we are introduced to His atoning sufferings. Everything else revealed the malice of the human heart, but now we must penetrate the darkness to learn what it meant for Him the Holy One, to bear away our sin.

Whatever His accusers may have said, He was wounded for [on account of] our transgressions and He was bruised for [on account of] our iniquities; such is the force of the twice repeated preposition. *Pierced* might even be a better word than wounded; it calls to mind the nail wounds and the spear thrust. But these were only the outward symbols of a greater piercing, for the wrath of God, like a sword, pierced His very soul, and caused Him to cry out, "My God, My God, why hast thou forsaken me?"

The prophet says, *He was bruised*, that is to say, *He was crushed.* On the way from the judgement hall to the hill of Calvary He was crushed beneath the weight of the cross, but this again was only a token of the crushing He endured when the load of human sin was laid on Him. This must be the meaning, for later in the song the prophet expressly states, "Yet it pleased the Lord to bruise Him; He has put Him to grief" (v.10).

Scripture speaks of God chastening His people as a father chastens his child. All such chastening is corrective, and through it the Lord seeks to draw back again to Himself any who may have strayed from His will. The chastisement that fell on Christ, however, was different. It was penal in character. All the punishment that had to be endured, that we might have peace with God, was endured by Christ on the cross. The punishment that wrought our peace was caused to fall on Him.

Whatever curse was mine, He bore,
The wormwood and the gall;
There in that lone mysterious hour,
My cup, He drained it all.

The prophet then summarises the vicarious nature of the sufferings of Christ like this, *and with His stripes we are healed.* It is interesting to link the close of this verse with its beginning: "He was wounded" and "We are healed." His was all the suffering, for *He was wounded*; and now ours is all the blessing, for *We are healed.* We might also note that the sufferings are in the past tense. But while the sufferings are past the blessing remains; for it says, we *are* healed. For all who have believed, heaven is already begun.

Ne'er again shall God Jehovah,
Smite the shepherd with the sword;
And ne'er again shall cruel sinners,
Set at nought our glorious Lord.

The Scope of the Atonement

The final verse of this third stanza centres on those for whom the Saviour suffered. The verse distills the very essence of the entire chapter. It begins with *all we* and it ends with *us all.* It identifies the ground on which all Israel will be saved in a future day, and it shows the basis of salvation today for all who have the faith of Abraham, even though they may not be physically descended from Abraham.

The phrase, *All we like sheep have gone astray* is one with which we have become very familiar. Because of this it would a pity to alter it even in a single word. However, "all we *like a flock* have gone astray" might more adequately convey the meaning. Each of us is part of a total family, the human family, which is alienated from God because of Adam's sin. But Isaiah will not allow us to simply blame our lostness on our first parents. He insists that *we have turned every one to his own way.* There is a personal culpability on our part. We all like to do our own thing, we have all gone our own way.

Happily, that is not the final word, for the prophet goes on to say, *And the Lord laid upon Him the iniquity of us all.* Here we have the whole gospel. Christ became our substitute on the cross. He took our place and stood in our stead. When He became the sin-bearer, the total weight of our iniquity was laid upon Him. In all this, God Himself was the supreme actor. Atonement could not have been accomplished by anything man might have done. It was the LORD who laid on Him the iniquity of us all. The atonement is altogether a divine accomplishment.

All our sins were laid on Jesus,
Jesus bore them on the tree.
God who knew them laid them on Him,
And believing we are free.

Universalism, the idea that all will eventually be saved, is not taught in this verse. It teaches rather that none need perish. And this is the basic impulse of all true gospel preaching. This verse reveals the foundation of the great commission to "Go into all the world and announce the glad tidings to every creature" (Mark16:16). We actually do have good news for *every creature*. But the message must be believed, and the Saviour must be received. The down side of this matter is very solemn, for it declares that "he who believes not the Son shall not see life, but the wrath of God abides on him" (John 3:36).

The Meaning of Imputation

Imputation, a foundational truth of Christianity, is forcefully brought to our notice in this verse. Scripture teaches three dimensions to this doctrine. First, there is the imputation of Adam's sin to us. (See Rom.5:12-21.) We commit sins because we are already sinners. This propensity towards sin, which is native to us all, has been passed down through the generations from our first parents. It comes naturally to little children to do what is wrong, but they must be painstakingly trained to do what is right. Of course, the ultimate proof that all are involved in the first man's sin is the fact of physical death.

In the second place, there is the imputation of our sin to Christ, "All we like sheep have gone astray ... *and the Lord has laid on Him the iniquity of us all.*" (See also 2Cor.5:21.) The point we have now reached in this verse clearly sets forth the first and second parts of imputation. The final dimension to this tremendous truth is the imputation of divine righteousness to all who believe on the Saviour's name. This righteousness is spoken of as the garment of salvation which is applied to believers at the point of conversion. It is the only garment in which we can find acceptance before God. Imputation is a term we have allowed to slip too easily from our vocabulary and, as a result, we have been very greatly impoverished.

Jesus, thy blood and righteousness
My beauty are, my glorious dress!
'Midst flaming worlds, in these arrayed,
With joy shall I lift up my head.

Bold shall I stand in that great day,
For who ought to my charge shall lay?
Fully through these absolved I am
From sin and fear, from guilt and shame.

The *Fourth Song*

Stanza No. 4

He was oppressed, and He was afflicted

If the third stanza of this song proclaims the sufferings of Christ in their substitutionary character, then this fourth stanza emphasises the profound silence of the sufferer. *He was oppressed, and He was afflicted, yet He opened not His mouth* (v.7). The latter phrase is repeated at the end of the verse.

We must first ask, what did it mean for Him to be oppressed and afflicted? To say that He was 'harassed' might better convey the meaning. Perhaps the greatest instance of this was in the final twenty four hour period before His death. During that period the Lord Jesus was arraigned before no fewer than six tribunals. He stood three times before the Jews and after that, three times before the Gentiles.

The Servant's Harassment

Following His arrest in the garden the Lord Jesus was brought to stand before Annas, the father-in-law of Caiaphas, who was high priest that year (John18:13). Then He was sent bound to Caiaphas himself (John18:24). After that He appeared before the Sanhedrin (Luke22:66). And when He was handed over to the Gentiles, He stood first before Pontius Pilate who sent Him to appear before Herod. Herod in turn, sent Him back to Pilate; who in the end, delivered Him to be crucified.

And yet through it all *He opened not His mouth.* Under the pressure of all that harassment and the contradiction of sinners that He endured, not one word of protest escaped our Saviour's lips. What an example of patience and forbearance He has given us, and we do well when we follow in His steps

And what a rebuke that silent sufferer is to any who might be tempted, at the slightest provocation, to assert themselves and insist upon what they judge to be their rights. The protest movement has become very popular in the ways of the world, but Christians should take their cue from Him who left us such an example.

As a lamb to the slaughter

The two figures of a *lamb led to the slaughter*, and of a *sheep before her shearers,* will readily appeal to all who have a farming background. The double figure must be understood in two ways. First, we must think of these things by way of comparison and then, by way of contrast. Unlike the pig which will raise such a din, the lamb will go silently to the slaughter. The sheep in the hands of the shearer, often receives very rough treatment; its flesh will even be torn at times, yet it lies there, quiet and still. All this was reflected in the man in the seamless robe who, before Pontius Pilate, "answered him never a word, insomuch that the governor marvelled greatly" (Matt. 27:14).

Besides the comparison there is a contrast too in these figures. When a lamb is led to the slaughter and a sheep to the shearer, both are ignorant of their fate. But when the Lord Jesus trod the Calvary road, He did so in the fullest possible understanding of what lay ahead. As the cross loomed before Him, He could say, "to this end was I born, and for this cause came I into the world, that I should bear witness to the truth" (John 18:37).

On an earlier occasion, when in Caesarea Philippi, and following Simon Peter's great confession and the first mention of the future church, the Lord Jesus "began to show unto His disciples, how He must go to Jerusalem, and suffer many things from the elders and chief priests and scribes, and be killed, and be raised again the third day" (Matt.16:21). Beyond any doubt, the death of the cross was entirely volountary, there was nothing at all of coercion about it.

There was one who was willing to die in my stead,
That a soul so unworthy might live.
And the path to the cross He was willing to tread,
All the sins of my life to forgive.

Jesus Alone

That unique occasion was also marked by a silence of a different and more sinister kind. *Who shall declare His generation* (v.8). This phrase is not easy to understand. Scholars, after careful study, are divided in their opinions. There seems to be good grounds for rendering it, *not one of His generation declared in His favour*. In the presence of that kind of harassment and manifest injustice the silence of His contemporaries was deafening. Yet the silence was such that not a single word was spoken in His defence.

For the judge to pronounce the prisoner innocent, and then, as a matter of political expediency, to commit that same prisoner to be crucified, made the whole scene a travesty of even the most elementary justice. This seems to be the idea behind the words *He was taken from prison and from judgement.* The preposition means *apart from* rather than *away from*. Prison and judgement represent the due processes of law, but these were set aside so that the trial of Jesus Christ was turned into a legal caricature, it was a parody of the most basic concepts of justice.

When Jesus was cut off out of the land of the living, He not only stood silent, He also stood alone. The whole scene is a reminder of David's words, when with relentlessly fury king Saul pursued him in the wilderness he said, "I am like a pelican ... like an owl of the desert. I watch, and am like a sparrow alone upon the housetop" (Psa. 102:6,7). And again, "I looked on my right hand, and beheld, but there was no man that would know me. Refuge failed me; no man cared for my soul" (Psa. 142:4).

Alone, alone,
He bore it all alone;
He gave His life to save His own,
He suffered, bled and died alone.

A Higher Purpose

Isaiah is always careful to keep before our minds that a higher purpose was being served in all that was associated with the trial and death of Jesus Christ. The first disciples too, in the midst of their persecutions, were strengthened by this knowledge. They made their prayer to God and remembered that, "Of a truth against your holy child, Jesus, whom you have anointed, both Herod, and Pontius Pilate, with the Gentiles, and the people of Israel, were gathered together, to do whatever your hand and your council determined before to be done" (Acts 4:27,28). A supreme purpose was being served in the cross of Christ. For even in Calvary's darkest hour, the Sovereign Lord was working all things after the counsel of His own will.

With prophetic insight Isaiah says of the Saviour, He was cut off out of the land of the living. And yet he insists, and we must never forget, that it was for the transgression of *my people* He was stricken. The expression *'my people'* needs some unpacking. Whatever does it mean, and how was it fulfilled?

Caiaphas

To help us understand these things we might recall, how many of the Jews believed on the Lord Jesus when Lazarus was raised from the dead. At that time the the chief priests and the Pharisees, being greatly troubled, took counsel and said, "What do we? For this man does many miracles. If we let Him thus alone, all men will believe on Him; and the Romans will come and take away both our place and nation" (John11:47,48). It was just at that point, something of great importance was spoken by Caiaphas, the High Priest, and what he said takes us to the heart of Isaiah's phrase.

To his co-conspirators the High Priest declared, "You know nothing at all, nor consider that it is expedient that one man should die for the people, and that the whole nation perish not" (John11:49,50). This statement was a definite prophecy and the context makes plain that Caiaphas was the unwitting mouthpiece of God when he uttered those words. "He prophesied that Jesus should die for that nation; and not for that nation only, but that also He should gather together in one the children of God that were scattered abroad" (John11:51,52).

For the Nation and for the World

While there were many significant dimensions to the death of the Lord Jesus, we know that He died for the nation of Israel in a quite specific sense. This seems to be what Isaiah had in mind when he said, it was for the transgression of *my people* He was stricken. And yet the prophecy of Caiaphas predicted ramifications in the death of Christ that reached beyond the nation of Israel.

Peter summarised the scope of Christ's death when he declared, "For the promise is unto you, and to your children, [presumably, a reference to Israel] and to all that are afar off, [presumably, a reference to the Gentile world] even as many as the Lord, our God, shall call" (Acts 2:39). We know that Christ's death also has implications for heavenly places as well, so that its virtue extends beyond even the limits of our earthly sphere. (See Hebs.9:23.)

This allows us to see ourselves in the cross. Even if we are not part of the Jewish race we can rejoice in the knowledge that Jesus was wounded for *our* transgressions and that He was bruised for *our* iniquities. It is virtually certain that Caiaphas and his people had no understanding of the momentous drama in which they had become involved. But of this we can be satisfied: Calvary was not an afterthought, something introduced by God to meet an unforeseen emergency. The cross had long been anticipated, hence the apostle Paul could write, "Christ died for our sins *according to the scriptures*" (1Cor.15:3).

Overruling Providence

All this is confirmed in the final verse of this fourth stanza. *He was assigned a grave with the wicked.* But in the overruling providence of God, *He was with the rich in His death* (v.9 *n.i.v.*). Having been condemned to a felon's death on a felon's cross it was assumed that He would find a felon's grave. His final resting place would be some shallow hole in some valley of Gehenna, it mattered not.

Joseph of Arimathea

But the scripture cannot be broken, and at the precise moment of His dying a man stepped forward, someone we had not before encountered in the gospel narratives. We know practically nothing of Joseph of Arimathea either before or after his immortal act. We are simply told how He went to Pilate and begged the body of Jesus, and with the help of Nicodemus, he took it down from the cross and laid it in his own new tomb. It was a tomb wherein no body had yet been laid. Beyond noting that he was a rich man, scripture tells us little about him. Unquestionably, we can say that he was God's man, in God's place, at God's time and for God's purpose.

It has often been pointed out that in the original text the word '*wicked*' is plural, whereas the word '*rich*' is singular. He was assigned a grave with *the wicked ones* but He was with *a rich one* in His death. It would not have done, for just one thief to have been crucified alongside our Saviour. And so the historian is careful to record that "They crucified Him, and the malefactors, one on the right hand, and the other on the left" (Luke 23:33). Clearly, a higher purpose was being fulfilled by a higher power in the cross of Christ. God was at work and none could stay His hand?

And only through that silent sufferer could that purpose be fulfilled. For of Him alone it could be said, "*He has done no violence, neither was any deceit in His mouth*" (v.9). A man's whole life is bound up in his deeds and his words. On both counts our Lord's life was impeccable. For this reason, He alone was worthy. Subsequently, God confirmed that tremendous fact by highly exalting Him, and by giving Him a name that is above every name. And all who love Him are ever ready to confess that He is also worthy of their best, and to accord Him the preeminent place in their lives.

The *Fourth Song*

Stanza No 5

Yet it pleased the Lord to bruise Him

The final part of this fourth song is an ocean into which all the other parts, like rivers, empty their fullness. Practically every major theme already referred to, is touched on again in these final verses. The *King James version* begins this section with the words, "*Yet it pleased the Lord to bruise Him, He has put Him to grief*" [*caused Him to suffer*]. The Servant King suffered many things from men and even from devils, but our redemption was accomplished by the sufferings He endured at the hands of God.

Having said that, this statement, taken at its face value, might almost seem to suggest that the Father found some sadistic-like pleasure in punishing His Son. But this was not so, indeed, even the suggestion of such a thing is absurd. The same expression is found again at the end of the verse, where it is rendered, "*The pleasure of the Lord shall prosper in His hand.*"

Paul used similar language when He referred to God's purpose as *the good pleasure of His will* (Eph.1:5). That all these references have in view the eternal purpose of God is clear from another rendering of Isaiah's words, "Yet it was the Lord's will to crush Him ... and the will of the Lord shall prosper in His hand" (*n.i.v.*).

The Centrality of the Cross

In one grand sweep this verse brings before us the centrality of the cross in the outworking of the divine programme. God was not wrongfooted by man's sin. He was not taken unawares by the catastrophe in Eden. All our need had been foreseen and the remedy incredibly foreordained. The plan of redemption was established from the foundation of the world. (See Rev.13:8.) That plan was to have its strategic centre in the cross, and in its outworking God would cause His Son to suffer.

Like the song itself, the verse encompasses the two advents of Christ. "*It pleased the Lord to bruise Him.*" This was central to the first advent. And that "*the pleasure of the Lord shall prosper in His hand,* will be the grand purpose of the second advent. The cross is the basis of all God's saving work; in the past and in the future as well as in the present. Israel's future salvation as a nation and the blessing of the Gentile nations in the millennial kingdom will all derive from the cross.

An Offering for Sin

There is some ambiguity about the first pronoun in the next phrase. Some understand it to read, "*When you* [Lord] *shall make His soul an offering for sin*" (v.10). This would certainly be in keeping with what has gone before, and would underline the Father's involvement in the sufferings of the Son. Others see the pronoun as referring to the sinner who comes to rest by faith on that one great sacrifice for sins. Both these views could well be sustained by the text and both are compatible with the truth of the gospel.

Some scholars, however, prefer to render the phrase "When His soul makes an offering for sin." (See Motyer on Isaiah. p.439 *i.v.p.*) This would certainly be in keeping with the statements that follow and it would serve to emphasise the voluntary nature of the Saviour's death. No man took His life from Him; He had power to lay it down, and He had power to take it again. Many had suffered death by crucifixion and many have since suffered martyrdom. But when Jesus died, His death was without parallel. His very soul transformed itself into an offering for sin.

Another interesting thing in this verse is that the word used for *sin* is normally translated *trespass*, as in the trespass offering. The trespass offering was one of the five principle offerings in the Levitical system. Its distinguishing and special feature was that it viewed sin as a debt needing to be paid. We are familiar with this idea for as we ramble in the countryside we are often confronted by a notice which says, "Trespassers will be prosecuted."

The trespass offering required reparation to be paid in full, and then, in addition, a fifth part was to be added. (See Lev.5.) If the debt amounted to 100 dollars, the total indemnity would then amount to 120 dollars. Only the Lord Jesus could comprehend the debt of sin and none but He could pay sin's price. And when the weight of human sin was laid on Him, Jesus paid it all. Such was the surpassing excellence of His atonement, He paid into the bank of Heaven a ransom, sufficient to meet the need of all who will repent and believe the gospel.

The Dying Penitent

The next phrase, *He shall see His seed* is also full of meaning. It would appear that at the precise time when Jesus offered Himself as the great trespass offering, this prediction too was fulfilled. If this is so, then it must surely refer to the penitent thief. How extraordinary it is that more than seven hundred years before the event, the prophet could have foreseen the cross in such astonishing detail.

The dying of Jesus was like a corn of wheat falling into the ground that it might bring forth fruit. As He looked on that dying penitent the Lord Jesus saw, personalised in him, the great harvest that would yet be reaped from His death. Believers of this church age are said to be, "a kind of firstfruits of His creatures." (James 1:18) In addition, in the age to come, a work of grace will be extended to national Israel, and so "all Israel shall be saved" (Rom.11:26). Later still, amid the glories of the millennial kingdom, the nations of the Gentiles will be brought into blessing in association with restored Israel (Rev.21:24).

In the hour of His deepest anguish the Lord Jesus could see all true believers of this present age, and of every other age in the face of that dying penitent. Both the writer and the reader, together with "all who in every place call upon the name of Jesus Christ our Lord," were before Him in that strange character who first railed on Him, and then repented, and finally owned Him as his Lord.

But is this real? Can it all be true? Or is it just so much theory? Is it just so much wishful thinking? The next phrase shows how substantial it actually is: "*He shall prolong His days.*" Here we have a clear reference to the resurrection of Christ on the third day. There is an obvious difference between how we use this expression in common parlance today, and how the prophet used it. We speak of a man's days being prolonged while he is still alive. But here the term is used of one who had already died.

A Risen Saviour

For the first disciples this scripture must have been heavy with mystery during the period that followed the crucifixion. But then on the third day, that glad day of the Saviour's resurrection, what light must have shone into their hearts from this ancient lamp. And what joy and consolation fill our hearts today through the knowledge that Jesus is alive. "If Christ be not risen, then is our preaching vain ... and your faith is vain, you are yet in your sins ... but now is Christ risen ... " (1Cor.15:14-20).

Christ is risen! Hallelujah!
Risen our victorious Head.
Sing His praises! Hallelujah!
Christ is risen from the dead.

Like the incarnation, the resurrection of Jesus Christ is not an end in itself for it too has an eschatological dimension. His first advent was always intended to prepare for a second, when He who is now His people's intercessor and advocate and the Head of the church, will return as Israel's King and as the world's Judge. All these offices required that He should rise from the dead. It was just not possible, therefore, that death could hold Him. And in raising His Son from the dead, God has given assurance unto all men that the pleasure of the Lord will ultimately prosper in His Servant's hand. (See Acts 17:31.)

Justification

Finding the sense of the middle part of verse eleven is not easy either. "*By His knowledge shall my righteous servant justify many.*" Some have oversimplified this and made it to read, 'by their coming to know Him shall my righteous servant justify many.' While such a rendering does no violence to the main thrust of the gospel, it does not seem to accurately reflect the text. The reference here is not to our knowledge of Him but to His own peculiar knowledge.

This verse is in three parts, and it will help us if we can first understand the other two parts. The final part is really an exclamation, "*for* [can't you see] *He shall bear their iniquities*!" The Lord of Glory became the Lamb of God in order to bear away the sin of the world. The hymn writer proclaimed, "*All our iniquities on Him were laid,*" and this is the ground of our justification, for we are "justified by His blood" (Rom.5:9).

Over against that, the first part of the verse brings us to the other side of the cross, it shows us Christ surveying, with total satisfaction, the results of His sacrifice. "*He shall see of the travail of His soul, and shall be satisfied.*" He is able to see that the purpose of His death has been fully accomplished. This seems to be the specific knowledge referred to in the middle part of the verse.

Another prophet inquired, "The heart is deceitful above all things, and desperately wicked; who can know it?" (Jer.17:9) The reality is, that only God can fathom the depravity that is native to the human heart. And the Lord Jesus knows what it is, for He is God; and for the same reason He also knows the holiness of God. It is by knowing the one and the other, and by knowing specifically, that His death has bridged the gulf between them, that He is now able to declare righteous all who come to Him in repentance and faith. This knowledge enables Him to justify believing sinners, without compromising His righteousness in any way.

The Servant's Triumph

The concluding verse of the song, as it appears in the *a.v.,* seems at first something of an anti-climax. "*Therefore I will divide Him a portion with the great, and He shall divide the spoil with the strong*" (v.12). After all that has already been said, and allowing the widest possible margin, shall our Servant King, in the end, simply take His place among the great ones of earth, and do no more than divide the spoil with the strong? Can it possibly be that in the final analysis, He is no greater than Mohammed, no greater than Buddha, no greater than the prophet of Bai'hi?

'I will apportion to Him the many, and He will apportion, as spoil, the strong' might be a better rendering of the text. (See Motyer on Isaiah p 442. *i.v.p.*) In the first stanza of this song, reference is made to *kings* and to *nations*; and now this verse seems to point to the fulfilment of what is prophesied there. Having seen the Lord Jesus first in His death and then in His resurrection, we are now transported into the future to see Him in His coming glory.

In that day, the day of His return, the Father will say to the Son, "Ask of me, and I will give you the nations for your inheritance, and the uttermost parts of the earth for your possession" (Psa.2:8). That coming day was anticipated by the prophet Daniel as the time when "the God of heaven shall set up a kingdom, which shall never be destroyed" (Dan.2:44).

And the Patmos Seer, when the seventh trumpet sounded, heard great voices in heaven, saying, "The kingdoms of this world are become the kingdom of our Lord, and of His Christ, and He shall reign forever and ever" (Rev.11:15). All these scriptures will have their full and unequivocal definition in that day.

Standing alone, without peer or rival, our Servant King will claim His inheritance. The kings of the earth will be in His hands, as spoil in the hands of a victor. He will be publicly manifested in the amazing uniqueness of His person and the whole earth will gaze on Him with surprise and astonishment. With bated breath kings will gape on Him, and holding nothing back every knee will bow, and every tongue will confess, that Jesus Christ is Lord, to the glory of God the Father.

Four Reasons for His Reward

Four reasons are now given as the grounds for the reward just announced. We have stressed that everything in the spiritual realm has been established in the cross, and now we read that the coming triumph of Christ is likewise based on His death. This is stated here in a fourfold way;

1. **He poured out His soul unto death;**
2. **And He was numbered with the transgressors;**
3. **And He bore the sin of many,**
4. **And made intercession for the transgressors.**

(1) ***He Poured out His soul unto death***

Some scholars tell us that this phrase should be rendered, 'He bared His soul unto death.' He kept nothing back. But perhaps it is best to think of the phrase in terms of the Old Testament *drink offering*. In the Levitical system there were five principal offerings; and besides these there were others, which were usually offered alongside one or more of the principal offerings. The drink offering was one of those secondary offerings. Significantly, it was never drunk, it was always poured out.

The drink offering came into prominence in connection with the morning and evening sacrifices. These particular sacrifices consisted of a burnt offering and a meal offering over which was poured the drink offering. The two principal offerings, taken together, speak of the perfect life of Christ which was yielded up to God. The drink offering, therefore, is linked in the first place to the life of the Lord Jesus, and to the laying down of that life in death upon the cross.

It is also relevant to note that the drink offering was an offering of wine, the actual amount varying according to the estimated value of the principal offering with which it was offered. Elsewhere in scripture, wine is viewed as a symbol of joy and gladness. (See Psa.104:15.) It was because of the joy set before Him, the Saviour endured the cross (Hebs.12:2). Whatever else may have been involved, this joy was the joy of ascending into the presence of God after He had passed through death. The sixteenth Psalm, quoted by

Peter at Pentecost, anticipated this: "In your presence is fullness of joy and at your right hand are pleasures for evermore" (Psa.16:11).

But besides being linked to His life and death, and to His resurrection and ascension, the drink offering also seems to have in view the coming glory of Christ. Although the instructions for it were given in the wilderness, they anticipated Israel's entry into the land. This offering had in view the time when the wanderings of His people would be ended and God would give them rest.

We know that this prospect, so soon to be realised for that generation, also looked forward to millennial days. It anticipates for us the time when the church shall reign with Christ. And so we are confronted once again with the three views of the Lord Jesus that keep recurring in scripture. In the past dying for us, in the present living for us, and in the future coming to call us to Himself.

David's drink offering

Perhaps the most notable example of the drink offering was in connection with David at the cave of Adullam, although the substance in this instance was water and not wine. The Philistines had established a garrison in Bethlehem when David was in hiding with some of his most trusted followers. Some of his men overheard David express a longing for a drink of the water of the well of Bethlehem, which was by the gate. David's desire was enough for them: they broke through the Philistine lines, and brought back some of that water.

To David, however, the water represented the blood of men who had hazarded their lives for his sake. He saw in it a proof of their devotion and of their commitment to his person. For this reason it was sacred to him, and he would not drink it. He poured it out before the Lord.

To us the principal offerings in the morning and evening sacrifice speak quite clearly of what the Saviour has done, but the drink offering, added to them, seems to tell us why He did it. It was in love that Jesus came, and it was love, love to God and to us, that led Him to Calvary where He poured out His soul unto death.

T'was love that sought Gethsemane.
Or Judas ne'er had found Him.
T'was love that nailed Him to the tree,
Or iron ne'er had bound him.

(2) *He was Numbered with the Transgressors*

The voluntary character of our Lord's death seems to be the thought behind the second of these four statements, "*He was numbered with the transgressors*." A superficial reading might lead us to conclude that the Roman authorities had a list of names for each day's executions, and on the day in question, they found just two names listed. Both were thieves and malefactors and so they added to the list the name of Jesus Christ of Nazareth, and in this way He was numbered with the transgressors.

But this would be to miss the vital fact that our Lord's death was a voluntary act in which He allowed Himself to be numbered with the transgressors. Even as He stood before Pontius Pilate in the judgement hall, Jesus understood fully what silence in the presence of His accusers would inevitably involve. It would involve Him in a public procession to a place of execution. He also knew that His companions in that procession would be thieves and malefactors.

Of no reputation

He knew that this would involve, not just His life, but His reputation as well. Many a mother has sacrificed her life for her child, and her reputation as a mother has not been harmed, indeed it has been enhanced. But when Jesus suffered for us, He was not only laying down His life, He was laying His very reputation on the line as well. In the event, two others were led out with Him to be put to death, and they were criminals. The immediate effect of this in the perception of the bystanders, would be that all three were suffering the due reward of their deeds.

Confirmation of this is found in the records of the third gospel. Luke informs us of what happened immediately following the institution of the Lord's Supper, and just before the little company proceeded to the garden where He was arrested. Significantly, it was at that point Jesus said to the disciples, "This that is written must yet be accomplished in me, *And He was reckoned among the transgressors;* for the things concerning me have a fulfilment" (Luke 22:37). In applying Isaiah's prediction to Himself, the Lord Jesus, in this statement, gave a unique insight into His own understanding of what the prophet had written.

In an extended passage on the Saviour's self-humbling Paul wrote, "He made Himself of no reputation" (Phil.2:6). Whatever else this means it surely reminds us of Isaiah's phrase. And it seems to highlight how He allowed himself to be numbered with the transgressors. This text, therefore, had an immediate fulfilment in the cross when Jesus was lifted up between two common criminals. (See Mark 15:28.)

Identified with us

But the term is surely much broader than that, for we are the transgressors with whom the Saviour identified Himself. Just as Cain and Abel, at the beginning of the Old Testament, are representative of all who have ever lived, so those two thieves are representative men. Spiritual minds have always seen the whole world represented, and indeed personalised, in the two who were crucified with Christ: the one who received Him, and the other who rejected Him.

Christ's identification with us sinners had its first expression in His birth. He passed by the realm of angels, and because we are partakers of flesh and blood, He took part of the same, and so He identified Himself with us and with our humanity. (See Hebs.2:14.)

Veiled in flesh the Godhead see,
Hail the incarnate deity.

And then, during His earthly pilgrimage, and especially during His public ministry, He was always identifying Himself with sinners. This identification was the precise significance of His baptism. On one celebrated occasion He was described as the friend of publicans and sinners. And when He visited Jericho, and was entertained in the home of Zacchaeus, the by-standers spoke reproachfully of Him and said, "He is gone to be guest with a man that is a sinner" (Luke19:7).

But His identification with transgressors found its supreme expression in the cross. For there He took our place, and there He stood in the sinners stead. The substitutionary character of His death allows us now to say, "While we were yet sinners, Christ died for us" (Rom.5:8). Paul made this very personal to himself when he wrote, "The Son of God loved *me* and gave Himself for *me*" (Gal.2:20).

Simon Magus

In marked contrast to this self-humbling of the Lord Jesus, we read in the New Testament of three men who apportioned to themselves the trappings of deity. There was Simon Magus who proclaimed himself to be some great one, and not for a moment did he rebuke those who said, "This man is the great power of God" (Acts 8:9,10). Yet all the while he was in the gall of bitterness and his heart was not right before God.

Herod Agrippa

Herod Agrippa, the grandson of Herod the Great, was another. After the martyrdom of James, he sat one day upon his throne, arrayed in royal apparel, and made a great oration. With one consent the people cried out, "It is the voice of a god and not of a man" (Acts 12:20-23). He may have revelled in the adulation of the people, but before that day came to an end, he was no more. His body was eaten of worms and he died a miserable death.

Antichrist

In the last days another man will arise, called the man of sin, and often referred to simply as the antichrist. He will enter into the temple of God and, usurping the place of God, will demand for himself the worship that is due only to God. (See 2Thess.2:3,4.) From other scriptures we know that the whole world will go after this man until he is finally destroyed by the brightness of our Lord's second advent.

There is not even a syllable in the respective records of these three to suggest that any of them betrayed the slightest trace of self-effacement. But when to the cross we turn our eyes and gaze on Calvary, there we see one who was indeed God, and yet for our sakes He gave Himself up to death, even death on a cross, and in doing so He surrendered not only His life but also His reputation.

If we compare the world's acclaim for its own with its treatment of God's Son, it is easy to see how incongruous, and how utterly inconsistent it would be for us to profess love for Christ, and at the same time to be dominated in heart and mind by the things of the world.

(3) ***He Bore the Sin of many***

This statement immediately raises a vexed question. How many did Christ die for? Here we must keep very close to what the scriptures actually say. Otherwise we will fall into the trap of trading off one school of theology against another. The phrase itself is in line with the Saviour's words at the institution of the Lord's Supper. He said, "This is my blood of the new testament, which is shed for *many* for the remission of sins" (Matt.26:28). Some insist that these references restrict the atonement to a certain limited number, whom they identify as the elect. But other scriptures seem to invest the atonement with a much wider significance.

For instance, Paul wrote to Timothy his son in the faith, "God, our Saviour, will have all men to be saved, and to come to the knowledge of the truth. For there is one God, and one mediator between God and men, the man, Christ Jesus, who gave Himself *a ransom for all*, to be testified in due time" (1Tim.2:3-6). In similar vein the apostle John witnessed to Jesus Christ the Righteous and said, "He is the propitiation [satisfaction] for our sins, and not for ours only, but also *for the sins of the whole world*" (1John 2:2).

The Lord's forerunner, John the Baptist, looked upon the Saviour one day as He walked and said, "Behold the Lamb of God, who taketh away *the sin of the world*" [the *cosmos* world] (John 1:29). All are agreed that the elect are those who are saved out of the *cosmos* world. If this is so, it follows that, according to the Baptist's view, the atoning work of Christ is not to be limited as some theology tends to limit it. On the contrary, it has implications for the whole wide world.

That this argument has generated more heat than light scarcely needs to be reported. This may very well be because the battle has been fought by both sides on the basis of a false premise. Often in scriptue *the many* is an expression set over against *the one*. "For if through the offence of *one, many* are dead, much more the grace of God ... by *one* man, Jesus Christ, has abounded unto *many*" (Rom.5:15) Again, "For as by *one* man's disobedience *many* were made sinners, so by the obedience of *one* shall *many* be made righteous" (Rom.5:19).

The Great Day of Atonement

The New Testament parallel to Isaiah's phrase is found in the epistle to the Hebrews. And it may provide the key to the whole controversy. There we read, "So Christ was once offered to bear *the sins of many*" (Hebs.9:28). The background to this statement is the great day of atonement in Israel. (See Lev.16.) On that occasion the High Priest acted, not on his own behalf, but on the behalf of others. He was acting, the *one* on the behalf of the *many*. The many in that instance was all Israel. But that did not mean that every Israelite automatically came into the good of the atonement. By no means, it was essential that each Israelite should afflict his soul, and do no work at all. Only in this way could he appropriate to himself the atonement made by one, yet made for all. (See Lev.16:29.)

The High Priest's annual ritual on the day in question was basically quite simple. He appeared first at the brazen altar where the sacrifice was slain. Then he carried the blood of atonement through the Holy Place and into the Holiest of all, which was known as the immediate presence of God. After appearing in the presence of God he then retraced his steps. As he came back through the Holy Place, he paused at the golden altar, before finally appearing again to the waiting people outside.

These three appearings of Israel's High Priest have their counterpart in Hebrews 9. Christ has appeared to put away sin by the sacrifice of Himself (v.26). He now appears in the presence of God for us (v.24). And He shall appear the second time without sin unto salvation (v.28).

When the Lord Jesus was once offered to bear the sins of many, He too, like the High Priest of Israel, was not acting on His own behalf but on the behalf of others. He, the one, was acting on behalf of the many. In this instance the many is the whole *cosmos* world. (See John1:29.) This does not mean that everyone is thereby saved. Not at all, for the atonement of Christ only avails for those who cease from their own works, and who repent and believe the gospel. These are like those Israelites who afflicted their souls and who did no work at all.

(4) *He Made Intercession for the Transgressors*

Besides preparing a place for His people, there are three great ministries presently occupying our Saviour in the heavenly sanctuary. He is there as a Mediator on the behalf of sinners. "There is one mediator between God and man, the man Christ Jesus, who gave His life a ransom for all" (1Tim.2:5,6). On behalf of believers He is there as our High Priest, and in this capacity, "He ever lives to make intercession for us" (Hebs.7:25). In addition to those ministries, He also represents us in the Father's presence as our Advocate. "These things are written that you sin not, but if any man sin, we have an advocate with the Father, Jesus Christ the righteous" (1John 2:1).

It is outside the scope of this volume to engage in an extended discussion of our Saviour's present session in heaven. But the verse before us requires that we should call attention to His intercessory ministry. Even before His death, certain events occured which gave insights into His present service. There is, for example, the quite extended record of what has become known as His high priestly prayer. (See John chapter 17.) This is required reading for all who wish to learn more of the Lord's present ministry in heaven.

I have prayed for you

A detailed record has also been preserved of the occasion when Simon Peter made his rather pretentious boast. He said, "Lord, I am ready to go with you, both into prison, and to death" (Luke 22:33). In reply Jesus delivered such a warning that the boaster should have been instantly alerted. And then He followed the warning with this wonderful statement, "Simon, Simon, Satan has desired to have you [all] ... but I have prayed for you [each]."

What a marvellous thing it is, that even when they are least conscious of it and when they can scarcely pray for themselves, believers are still being sustained by prayer. They have a High Priest "who ever lives to make intercession for them" (Hebs.7:25). In both these instances, John and Luke present us with telling foreshadowings of our Saviour's present ministry.

The final words of this fourth song, *He made intercession for the transgressors*, are usually taken to have been fulfilled in the oft quoted prayer on the cross, when the Lord Jesus prayed for the soldiers who crucified Him. He said, "Father forgive them for they know not what they do" (Luke 23:34). However, it is unlikely that that prayer, precious as it was, exhausted the range of the intercession anticipated here by Isaiah.

It is always helpful to think of ourselves as the transgressors who are the subjects of Christ's intercessions and to keep in mind that He engages in this remarkable ministry as a man, a risen and glorified man. As a man He trod this earth in human weakness, entering into so many situations of human infirmity and adversity. And now, having identified Himself with us in all our distresses, He is able as our Great High Priest, to minister to us timely grace equal to our need.

Several times we have called attention to the three views of Christ that are repeatedly before us in the sacred scriptures. We have found this particularly true in the Servant songs. And here we have them again in this final verse. It begins with what Christ will do in the future and it also describes what He has done in the past. But at its close, it calls attention to what He is doing now during this present interval in time. The risen and ascended Lord Jesus is actively engaged in a great intercessory ministry in the presence of God. He is making intercession for the transgressors.

And so the final stanza of this fourth song ends like the first. (See Isa.52:15.) It brings us to the day of His glory and it lets us see the King in His beauty. In that day, the whole earth will look on in manifest astonishment, and every knee shall bow, and every tongue shall confess, that Jesus Christ is Lord, to the glory of God the Father. Amen and Amen.

Subject Index

T

U

W

Y